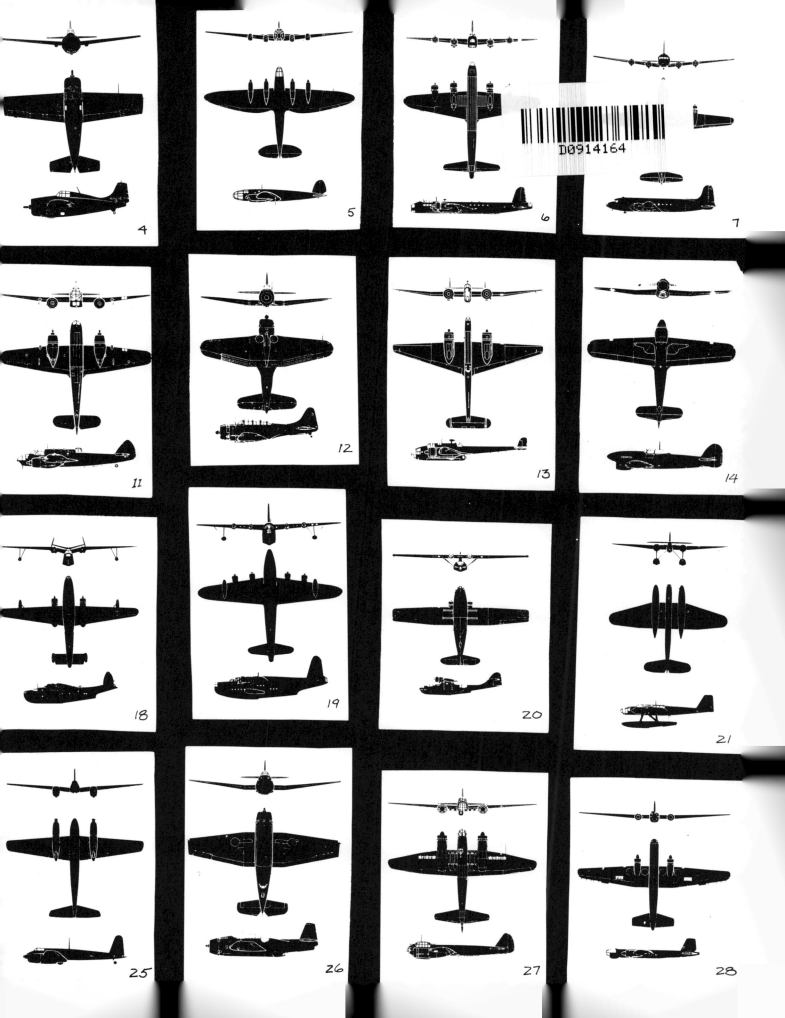

D0914164

TWO WINGS
and a
PRAYER

God grant me
the serenity
to accept the
things I cannot
change,
courage to change
the things I can,
& the wisdom
to know
the difference.

EX LIBRIS

Christmas 1984
To Dad from Lee-Ann

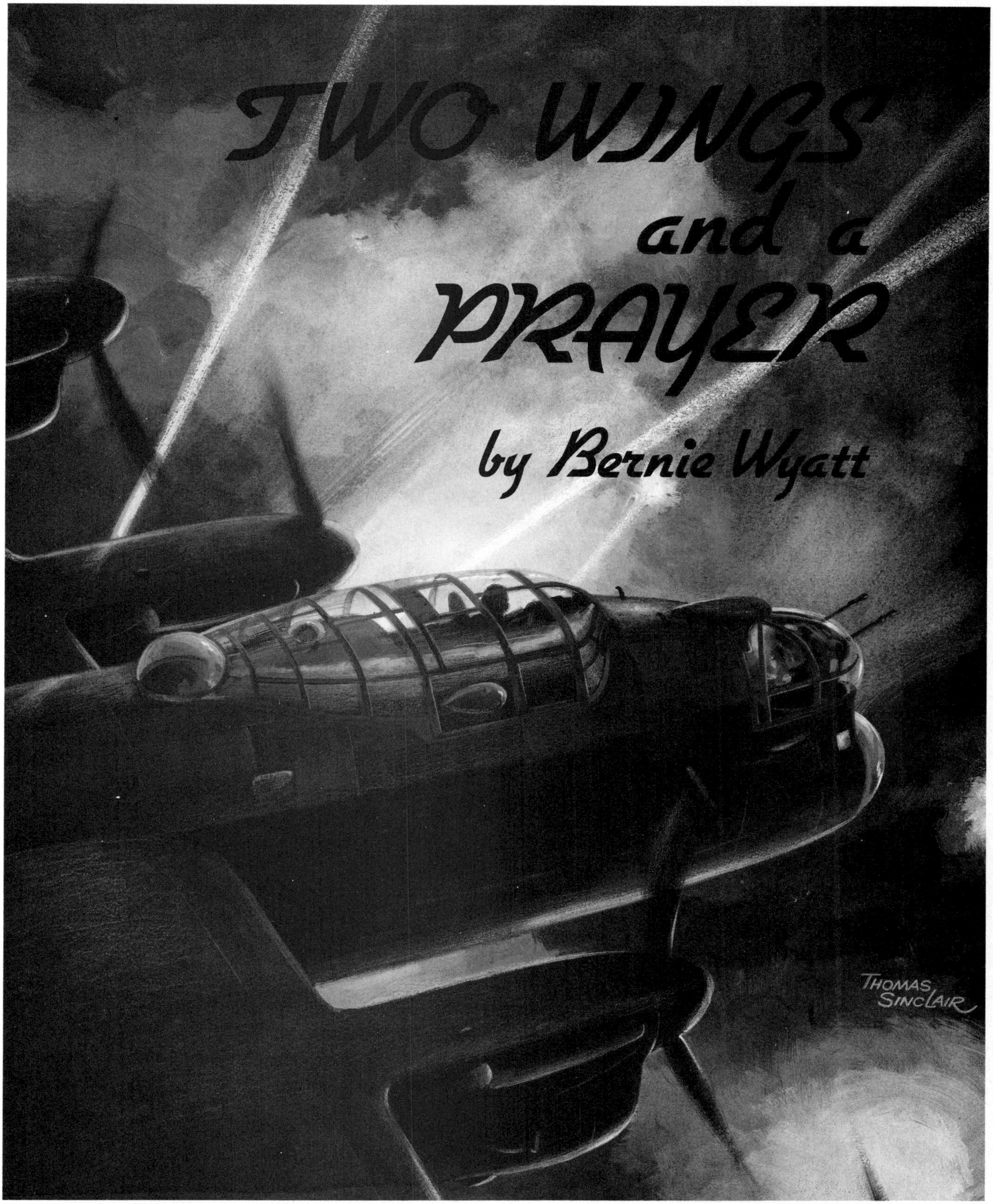
TWO WINGS
and a
PRAYER
by Bernie Wyatt
THOMAS
SINCLAIR

Canadian Cataloguing in Publication Data

Wyatt, Bernie, 1952-
    Two wings and a prayer

ISBN 0-919783-08-2

1. World War, 1939-1945 — Aerial operations,
Canadian.   2. World War, 1939-1945 — Personal
narratives, Canadian.   I. Title.

D792.C2W93 1984   940.54'4971   C84-098829-X

© Bernie Wyatt, 1984

Published by:
THE BOSTON MILLS PRESS
98 Main Street
Erin, Ontario N0B 1T0
(519) 833-2407

Winners of the
Heritage Canada
Communications Award

American Association
for State and Local History
Award Winner

Design by John Denison
Cover painting by Thomas Sinclair
Line drawings by Bernie Wyatt

Typeset by Linotext Inc., Toronto
Printed by Tri-Graphic, Ottawa

We wish to acknowledge the financial assistance of The Canada Council,
the Ontario Arts Council and the Office of the Secretary of State.

Introduction

Whenever World War II veterans get together, they love to talk about their war experiences. They tell stories. Funny stories, usually, because they like to talk about the good times and forget about the bad. I wasn't in the war, but I love to listen to these stories, especially the Air Force ones.

My dad did a hitch with the Royal Canadian Air Force for four years during the war. Two of those years were spent at No.16 SFTS, Hagersville, Ontario, where he was part of the ground staff. He had a favourite story, too. In April of 1983, I convinced my dad to write down two or three of his favourite stories for me so that I would have a record of them; and, he humbly agreed. After, I got to thinking that maybe, just maybe, there were other Air Force vets who were willing to relate some personal experiences.

At first, I never thought of publishing these accounts. That was the furthest from my mind. But I did notice the enthusiasm of the vets and my own friends when I mentioned what I was doing. A few people thought I was crazy, but not very many! After about three months of collecting stories, I decided I'd try to get the stories published. That was my goal.

Within this book are stories from over 50 different Canadian and American Air Force vets. Most of them permitted me to use their name, rank and serial number, while only a handful prefered I didn't identify them.

I would like to thank all these people for allowing me to print their recollections. And I'd also like to thank all the Canadian and American World War II veterans in general, for their participation in the war effort, although many of them feel that they played only a small part, they all contributed in the fight for personal freedom. My generation—the post-war "Baby Boom" kids—are reaping the benefits from their contribution.

I would like to dedicate this book to my father, whose favourite Air Force stories provided the incentive for collecting further stories.

Bernie Wyatt

Contents

B-24 Liberators over the Alps.
— *Bill Bruce (US Army Air Forces photo)*

Abbreviations

AOS — Air Observers School
BAAC — British Army Air Corps
Capt — Captain
CO — Commanding Officer
Cpl — Corporal
DFC — Distinguished Flying Cross
DSO — Distinguished Service Order
FC — Ferry Command
F/C — Flight Commander
F/L — Flight Lieutenant
F/O — Flying Officer (RAF and RCAF)
        Flight Officer (USAAF)
F/Sgt — Flight Sergeant
G/C — Group Commander
IFF — Identification Friend or Foe
ITS — Initial Training School
KP — work duty
LAC — Leading Aircraftman
Lt/Col — Lieutenant Colonel
M/Sgt — Master Sergeant
Op — combat mission
OTU — Operational Training Unit
P/O — Pilot Officer
POW — prisoner-of-war
RAAF — Royal Australian Air Force
RAF — Royal Air Force
RCAF — Royal Canadian Air Force
R/O — Radio Operator
RNVR — Royal Naval Volunteer Reserve
R&R — rest and relaxation
SFTS — Service Flying Training School
Sgt — Sergeant
S/L — Squadron Leader
S/Sgt — Staff Sergeant
Sub-Lieut — Sub Lieutenant
T/Sgt — Technical Sergeant
VE — Victory Europe (Victory over Germany)
VJ — Victory Japan (Victory over Japan)
WAAF — Women's Auxiliary Air Force
W/C — Wing Commander
WO1 — Warrant Officer first class
WO2 — Warrant Officer second class
USAAF — United States Army Air Forces
1st/Lt — First Lieutenant

*Bomb Group photo showing
bomb hits on Munich, Germany.*
— *Bill Bruce (US Army Air Forces photo)*

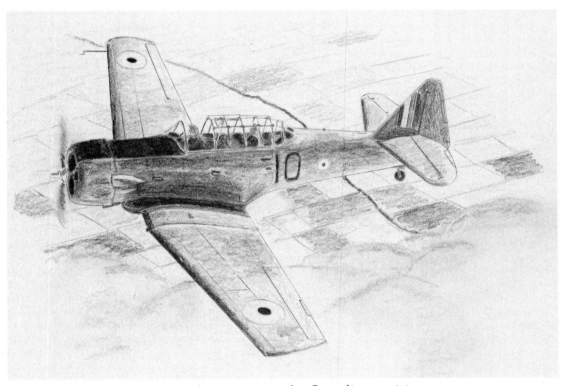

Harvard trainer over the Canadian prairies

IN TRAINING

He gave the sergeant my name!

We used to drop 'streamers'. I was on a refresher course; four weeks at Mt. Hope (Ontario) before I went overseas.

I was the wireless-operator on our plane and I'd turn the radio to the best jazz station I could find and the pilot and I would be singing and swinging away. Then we'd fly over Lake Ontario and dump out a roll of toilet paper. As the paper went down it would unravel and eventually turn into a 'streamer'. Then we'd chase it down and cut it up until nothing was left. Sometimes, when we'd get back to Mt. Hope, there'd be toilet paper all stuck in the cowlings. One time the CO was in the tower when we landed and he could see us taxiing by with all this white stuff on the front of our plane—it was a Yale, by the way—and he asked the other guys in the tower what that white stuff was. They knew but they wouldn't tell him. The mechanics knew too; but these poor guys were the ones who had to pull the stuff out of the engine cowlings. I wonder why that paper never burnt up in there.

I joined the RCAF at Kitchener and was sent to London. I reported to London in January of '42, and was given a big pile of tickets—I was being posted to Manning Depot in Edmonton, and that was 2,300 miles away.

Now, this was in the winter, but it wasn't too cold in Ontario. But when we got to Edmonton it was about 50 below, and there I was with no proper winter clothing! I had a scarf but no hat. Nothing like that. Heck, just going from your bunkhouse to go have supper in another building you'd have to cover your ears or else you'd freeze them off. And when we got inside you'd see the front of your coat all white from the frost.

When we were at Edmonton there were very few late-passes given. We learned to march and stuff like that, while they're trying to figure out what we wanted to be. It was a four-week course and you were given, maybe, one late-pass. Otherwise curfew was at 11 o'clock. If you didn't get in at 11 and you didn't sneak past the guard house, then you were put on KP duty.

When I was stationed in Winnipeg, we used to have supper around 6 o'clock, then we'd have to be back at 11 for roll call. So, for those few hours in between we used to end up in the wet canteen, drinking and blowing our money.

One night everybody got back in time for roll call except for one guy who was a few minutes late. The sergeant was not too happy with us, let me tell you. He gave us heck for being late and rowdy. Well, one guy in the back row couldn't take it anymore and yells, "Up yours!"

Now the sergeant was really mad! He stomped all the way to the back row and singles out this guy, then says to him, "What's your name?"

And he gave the sergeant my name! He says, "Roy Schmidt, sir."

But the dumb sergeant wasn't smart enough to ask him his regimental number because I'm the only one who knew that. Meanwhile, I was in the front row when all this was going on and didn't want to say otherwise because I didn't want to be a shmuck.

So next day, sure enough, I'm called out of parade and marched to the CO. The CO asked me if I talked back to the sergeant and I said, "No sir, it wasn't me. I don't know who said it but it wasn't me. If you call the sergeant, he'll be able to identify me and say I didn't do it."

Anyway, the sergeant came over and said, "Well, I don't know for sure because I was so mad. Yah, you look like the guy."

So, I got KP duty—seven days—washing dishes, with no leave. And that dirty guy who gave my name wouldn't even take half of it on me! I thought I might do three days of it, and he'd do the rest. But he didn't. I probably still have it on my record.

Finally, in 1945, I made it overseas. But do you know what day I left? The day the war ended, that's what! I still can't get my pension because of that. I was involved in the 'clean up' work after the war, so I put in my time, but I still can't get my pension.

F/O Roy Schmidt
RCAF
J48932

Pieces in The Wreckage

The winter of 1942 was horrible. The snow was up to your armpits and, boy, was it cold! I was only 19 years old at the time and stationed at Manning Depot in Toronto.

That winter we heard that a German prisoner escaped from one of those POW camps that were up north. So for our own protection, we were each given a 1903 Ross rifle which, by the way, didn't have a firing pin. We weren't even given any bullets.

Also at Manning that same winter, a flat-bed truck came on the property and parked at the back of the depot. On it was a mangled Harvard trainer that had crashed somewhere up north. We were given strict orders not to go near the truck or the Harvard. Well, back in those days when we were told not to do something, we'd just go out and do it anyway. In this case I wanted to check the plane out for any broken plexiglass that we could use. We used to take the plexiglass and carve out things like hearts and air-gunner wings, and send them to our parents for Christmas. When I was told by a fellow about this Harvard being on the property, I just had to get some glass from it. So I walked over to take a look.

As I got right up to it and looked around, I saw a shoe and a foot that, I guess, had once belonged to the pilot who died in the wreckage.

Cpl Jerry Campell
RCAF
186120

The Red Alert

My career in the Air Force was basically instructing in the British Commonwealth Air Training Plan. I spent considerable time at No. 7 AOS in Portage la Prairie, Manitoba, where I taught the students wireless-operating and Radio Direction Finding. At this station we flew Ansons and many hours were spent in the air teaching these students.

One of the things that immediately comes to mind during my stay on the prairies was the weather. It sure got cold! The Mark 1 Anson, which we used the first while, never really had a proper heating system. The plane was designed in Britain where it's warmer and they didn't take into consideration that the plane might be flown in Western Canada. The heating was exhaust gas by-passes which came through the cabin and that was all we had. Crude, but that was it back then.

And to relieve yourself there was a funnel that went out of the plane. On a cold night it would actually backfill because it didn't quite get out before it froze. But these things weren't suffering compared to what the fellows in combat were facing.

I remember one thing at Portage la Prairie that might be of interest.

If the guys on the base ever did a night or evening flight and got back around midnight, before the mess closed, they were given a scrip for a big meal of bacon, eggs, toast and coffee at the mess. I, for one, really enjoyed that meal. A few others must've enjoyed it too because they eventually made some counterfeit scrips. It got to be a big thing on the station. It all started out by someone stealing the signal officer's signature stamp, and from that they made a bunch of these scrips. Pretty soon there were more people in the mess than there were flying that night.

But all good things must end. After a while they found out what was going on. We were all confined to barracks and questioned, but nothing came of it. A few weeks later, after all this quieted down, the guys got out the phony scrips again.

In 1944 I was sent out to the west coast which was getting to be a serious front of operation due to the Japanese threat. I was assigned to the air-sea rescue part of a Canso squadron at Coal Harbour, B.C. No. 6 Squadron was the name.

Our motorboat was a big 90-foot vessel with a 60-foot beam and driven by a couple of 1,250 horsepower V-12's. It was called the Malecite and could go up to 60 knots! The crew consisted of a skipper, first-mate, first and second engineer, myself as first wireless, a second wireless, a cook and a deck hand. Every time the squadron put out to sea in search of submarines, we'd go out and wait for any distress calls.

During my tour there never were any distress calls but we did have a 'Red Alert'. It happened when the crew of an American bomber thought they saw the periscope and tower of a Japanese sub. Right away our squadron put out to sea and we all went racing out to the area to find a big Douglas Fir with a twisted branch sticking out of the water!

Cpl Bernie Klein
RCAF
R196271

The 'E' Flight instructors at No. 7 AOS, Portage la Prairie, Manitoba.
Cpl Bernie Klein is in the front row, second from the left.

By the Grace of God I missed being on it

One thing really stands out in my mind during the war and it happened in Las Vegas, Nevada. I was being trained as a navigator-gunner for B-29's, but we took the training on B-24 Liberators. I was supposed to fly this particular morning and I told my wife, who worked on another part of the base, that I'd be back at noon and then we'd go out for lunch.

Before we left I felt a sore throat coming on, and I went to see the doctor. He looked me over and told me I was grounded for the day. Well, now I had nothing to do. I walked into the barracks and noticed a poker game going on, so I joined in. By 11:30 I cleaned everybody out—thirty-eight bucks. Then I went over to see my wife.

When she saw me she said, "Oh, back already?"

"No, I never went. The doc grounded me. By the way, let's go see my plane come in and then we'll go for lunch." So off we went to take a look.

The B-24 came into view and made a turn to get closer to the runway, and right away I could see she's in trouble. One motor was out and just before touch-down the pilot made a very foolish mistake. Whenever an engine is out you never bank a plane to the side of a dead motor: you always bank it towards the good side. Otherwise, the drag will pull you right into the ground. Well, that's exactly what happened. The plane went straight into the ground and exploded! Everyone died on impact except the co-pilot, who died two days later. That was the plane that I was to be on! By the grace of God I missed being on it.

Dick Burg Dorf
USAAF
42021496

Dick Burg Dorf beside US Army trainer at base in Courtland, Alabama, May, 1944.

I was Getting to Almost Hate Facing People

In 1942 I was stationed at No. 1 Bombing and Gunnery School in Jarvis, Ontario. From there I was posted to Air Force Headquarters in Ottawa, where I was told I'd be going on a promotional tour in the United States.

I was to be part of an 8-man crew. The idea was to make a fund-raising tour and display a shot-down Messerschmitt 109 fighter plane for the American public—'Bundles for Britain' it was called in Britain, and in the States it was 'Bundles for Blue Jackets'. The public would look at the fighter while myself and another member handled the microphone. We would give a lecture and answer questions. It went on six days a week—10 AM to 10 PM. We each had 2 hours on and 2 hours off, and some of them were radio interviews; an experience I had never done before or since. But that's the way things were done in the Air Force: you were told to do something and you did it.

The rest of the crew members were as follows: the manager and co-manager, both from Paramount Studios in Hollywood, handled the display. The advance agent was from the Philadelphia Enquirer, and he arranged the bookings and press releases. A married couple from Chattanooga looked after the ticket sales. We also had a truck driver and a night watchman. Then there was myself, the only Canadian and the only one in uniform, representing the Air Force.

I caught up with the tour in Montgomery, Alabama, in early January of '42 and finished with them five months later, in the Mid-West, when the tour was postponed. Some of the cities we visited were Palm Beach, Houston, Oklahoma City, Topeka, Omaha, Des Moines, Springfield, Chicago and Milwaukee.

The history of this particular Me-109 was not substantiated, so I'll just tell you what was handed down to me. It was supposedly shot down over Kent, England in August, 1940, and had to make a crash landing. The plane was flown by a Luftwaffe airman named Karl Ebbighausen who had, up to that point, shot down five Allied planes—two French, two Dutch and one British. It was in pretty fair condition except for bent prop blades and a few scratches here and there. The armament included four machine guns and three cannons. The engine in it was a Daimler-Benz 12-cylinder, with about the same horsepower rating as the Rolls-Royce Merlin. The identification plate on the front end of the engine read: N1190 which stood for the frame number, and BF10912E which stood for the aircraft type.

When we reached a place, our advance agent would contact the nearest Air Force or military unit and ask for volunteers to set up the exhibit. So many would always volunteer that they couldn't accommodate them all. Those Americans were only too happy to get off Boot Camp and see an enemy fighter plane that they had heard so much about but had never seen.

Anyway, the plane was rolled out of the transport truck and onto the site—sometimes inside a building and other times in an enclosure or a tent. There was an admission charge to collect funds for the venture.

It was interesting work but I got tired of it after a while. The 6-day week, 10 AM to 10 PM, and the same questions over and over again were getting to be too much. I was getting to almost hate facing people. One of the questions they kept asking me was, "Why are the blades bent back like that?'

And I'd tell them something dumb like, "So they could cut their way through the jungles!"

F/Sgt W. W. Baron
RCAF (Ret'd)
2538

Glider Training

I came into the Army Air Corps as a corporal. Our training involved some tough, physical exercises, run-marches, etc., which were too tough for a few trainees and they dropped out. Our officers deliberately made it hard, to weed out the ones they didn't want.

They were tough in those days. We had three fellows in our Army group who had their RAF wings—they'd been kicked down. One man was flying Wellington bombers, but complained too much. He was a short fellow and had trouble reaching the controls. He wanted to fly fighters, where the controls were closer to him. His superiors didn't like to be told this so they transferred him to the Army.

After Preliminary Ground Training we went to Elementary Power Training flying Tiger Moths; a fun little single-engine trainer that was quite easy to fly. It would climb at 60 miles-per-hour and level at about 90. You could only get it into a spin by pulling the nose up until it stalled and then applying hard rudder. It would straighten out just by taking your hands and feet off the controls. Also, the Tiger Moth could take off with the pilot just handling the rudders.

During training our colonel, who was a man in his 50's, had wanted to fly. He took flying lessons and the first time he flew a Tiger Moth solo some of us were on the ground wondering if he'd ever get down. While the other students were ready to solo after six or eight hours it took him at least twenty.

He passed elementary training with us and then followed us into glider training. But the first time he got up and cast off he completely lost his way, crashed and killed himself. It was really a shame, but he was just too old to start flying.

Before I talk about glider training, I remember one other incident in power training. One pilot landed his Tiger Moth and walked out in front of the plane when the propeller was still turning. The only trouble was he walked right into the prop blade and down he went from the force. The blade hit him right on the head and a piece was knocked off the blade. As he got up the prop hit him again and down he went. I immediately came to the conclusion that he must've had an awfully hard skull.

Now came the glider training. We were told we'd be split into two groups. The larger group would be sent somewhere in Wales while the other would go to an RAF station in England. Well, my buddies and I—there were six of us who were all in the same flight—didn't want any part of Wales; we wanted to stay in England because we knew where that RAF base was and also knew it was close to big towns which had all the modern conveniences. We talked to the corporal who was handling the lists and with a little bit of persuasion managed to arrange for the six of us go to the smaller RAF station, where we started our glider training.

The elementary training glider was a two-seater and the instructor sat behind the pupil. This glider didn't have any brakes but it did have a wood skid below the nose. To come to a halt after landing the pilot had to gently push the nose down so that the skid rubbed along the grass.

On one of our exercises, the tug plane—in this case the Miles Master which was the British equivalent to the Harvard—would take us up to 8,000 feet and then you were on your own. You had to map-read your way back to base. After casting off, the glider would be trimmed for normal gliding speed and you'd make a gradual descent. On arrival over the airfield the rate of descent would be increased by the use of flaps to get rid of excess height. Once the glider was landed it would be brought to a halt using the skid board on the nose.

Another exercise was to try and spot-land the glider on a strip of cardboard 18 inches wide by 5 feet long. We got to be pretty good. We could touch down within a foot or so of the board. We could see the reasoning in this because in combat conditions you had to land your gliders in the right spots to be of any use to the ground forces.

Our first operational glider was called a Horsa which was named after some mythical god in Scandinavian folklore. Each glider would hold a pilot and co-pilot and there was always a co-pilot in the plane; even when you went solo. It was either a co-pilot or a bag of sand weighing as much as an average man, to balance the weight of the pilot.

I remember a funny thing that happened when I was with the group. There was an Irishman who was an explosives expert from the Spanish Civil War and who believed that crazy 'superior race' stuff that the Germans were teaching. (Ireland was neutral during the war but many Irishmen served in the British forces.) We had to do an exercise that went like this: our gliders would be towed to 2,000 feet, then we would cast off and take a sudden dive, reaching a speed of about 120 miles-per-hour, level off at 200 feet, come in at high speed close to the ground, supposedly to escape anti-aircraft fire, and finally land with proper flap. This Irishman, who was in his 30's and past his prime for flying, was the pilot and I was the co-pilot when we tried this procedure.

When we were free from the tow plane at 2,000 feet he took a dive and zipped along at high speed on the approach to the airfield. But he undershot and we headed straight for a mound of tarmac at the end of the airfield. We hit the tarmac with one wheel, knocking that wheel off and kept on going down the perimeter track right between rows of parked aircraft. As we lost speed, the wing that was minus the wheel dropped down and scraped the pavement, causing the glider to pull to one side and stop dead—right between two parked planes! The luck of the Irish.

It was getting close to D-Day so we were split into two groups. One group—Group A—had to be pushed through in a hurry and be ready for combat in France; Group B would be held up and complete the final training at a later date. I was in Group A to start but after some switching around I ended up in B. The fellow who switched with me, I later found out, was killed on D-Day. In fact, I never did fly in combat.

After completing our flying training, we were all posted to different operational squadrons, flying Horsas. After a year I was posted to Tarrant Rushton where they were flying the Hamilcar; a much bigger glider than the Horsa. Quite a few pilots were not keen to fly the Hamilcar because it was so much bigger and looked harder to handle, but I liked it. It had two flaps, that were about as big as a door, on each wing and the flaps acted like air brakes. The Hamilcar could carry ten tons of equipment—tanks, armoured trucks, men, radar supplies—and was usually towed by a Halifax bomber.

The runways at Tarrant Rushton were about a mile long and at either end of the runways was an undershoot and an overshoot; just in case the take-off and landing timing would be off. On the other side of the overshoot was a hedge and after that a valley. On one training procedure it appeared we weren't going to get off the ground because the gliders were really loaded down. The secret was to get the glider airborne in a hurry so that there was less drag on the tow plane and both could get off the runway. This was done by pulling back on the control column which in turn would lift the glider thereby decreasing the drag and helping the tow plane. It was teamwork. But this certain time the gliders were heavier than usual.

I was going to be the third one off so I kept my eyes glued to the first two. The first crew took off and started down the runway. I could see the glider wasn't lifting fast enough and they barely made it over the hedge. Down they went into the valley. We all held our breath but a few seconds later they appeared, flying out of the valley. The next crew takes off and the same thing happens. Now it came to me. I made up my mind, by this time, that I was going to get the glider into the air long before the hedge. But I didn't, and down I went, too.

Gliding was a great feeling. What I liked most was casting off at around 8,000 feet on a calm, sunny day and not even touching the controls. The only sound you'd hear was the hissing of the air as the glider cut through it. It would take about thirty minutes to come down, and I enjoyed every minute of it. What a sensation!

When I was in the Army and the Air Corps, the government looked after everything for you—food, clothing, medical, and other things. I always had money. Whenever I wanted to buy something I just went to my pocket and pulled out a pound note. Then, when the war ended and I took a civilian job, I was suddenly faced with a 20 percent cut in pay! It almost made me want to get back into the Army!

S/Sgt Les Willins
BAAC
7894475

The aircraft carpenter crew at No. 16 SFTS, Hagersville, Ontario. My father, Cpl Jack Wyatt, is in the middle of the back row.

THE FLYING SCHOOLS IN CANADA

Mosquito at Full-Throttle

I'd like to relate a couple incidents which happened at Hagersville, Ontario.

A Lysander from Jarvis Bombing and Gunnery School landed and came down the taxi strip intending to turn and park along-side a row of Ansons. But the Lysander's brakes failed and the aircraft sailed straight for one of our trainers. That poor thing—the Anson—didn't stand a chance. The Lysander's metal prop litterly gobbled up 10 feet of the Anson's wing, spitting splinters 40 feet in every direction.

A few months later, word was received that a Mosquito was to make a low-level pass over our airport. The ceiling was too low for student flying, so the whole station was on the lookout for this high-speed aircraft. All of a sudden we heard a plane, and upon tearing outside we caught a glimpse of the Mosquito as it swept across the field at full-throttle! Five or six seconds, and it was all over. That's all it took.

Cpl Jack Wyatt
RCAF
R150000

The Hagersville Crash

I was in the control-tower one day at Hagersville.

I was a pilot on the base but I was asked to sub in the tower because the other controller had to go into Hamilton. The work in the tower wasn't too hard because you didn't have to do much during the day flying, as we didn't have any radio communication. That was only during the night flying. During the day all you had to do was fire up a flare if two planes got too close; things like that.

As this particular Anson pilot, who was on his first solo flight, approached the runway he hit much too hard and bounced a good 10 feet in the air. Instead of letting the nose drop and making a landing he panicked and gave both engines full-throttle and by this time the aircraft was moving to the right—where the hangars and the control-tower were!

I was at the top of a set of stairs when I saw him coming and I was ready to jump down if I had to. The other controller ran out to the cat-walk that surrounded the tower which was a dumb thing to do; he wouldn't have any protection if the plane hit the tower.

The plane went by and all I could see was the entire bottom of the Anson because by this time the pilot had banked the plane to the right so he wouldn't hit the tower! As he did this he came back towards No. 2 hangar and scraped a corner of the roof with his right wing and the fuselage. Then he slid off the roof, hit a power pole and came to a stop.

The fire department came right away and foamed the Anson down. The pilot was shaken but, you know, he continued flying after that incident.

Another time, one Sunday morning, I was flying over Kitchener when the student pilot with me noticed some smoke coming out of one of the houses.

A pranged Anson at Hagersville. It is not the Anson that missed the control-tower, as related in the story.

Carl Cressman in front of a Mark II Avro Anson at No. 16 SFTS, Hagersville, Ontario.

We got a little closer and could see that it looked serious—a house was on fire! Normally a pilot couldn't fly any lower than 1,000 feet, except in an emergency, but this was an emergency. We always looked for an opportunity to fly lower than the limit. I buzzed the neighbourhood to try and get somebody out of bed—it was about 8 in the morning—so that they would notice the fire and get the fire department there. After buzzing a few times and making a heck of a racket, I looked down the street and could see the fire trucks coming. Somebody had called them.

A couple of days later my parents were reading the Kitchener paper and they noticed a heading that read, "HEADY AIRMEN SAVES BUILDING—Keeps Circling Until Resident Sees Fire in Apartment House." It didn't mention my name; but said an unknown pilot saved the house and its occupants. It also said the fire damage was about $3,000 or $4,000 to the roof.

F/O Carl Cressman
RCAF
J22271

Getting Lost on The Prairies

I was a student pilot at a base near Neepawa, Manitoba. When practising circuits at that particular base the student pilots had to concentrate on four things: watch for a certain red farmhouse and turn left; look for four trees and turn left; look for a wheat field and turn left; there in front of you should be the runway and you land. Nice and easy, right!

Well, one pilot lost his way and landed his Tiger Moth a hundred miles away. When he made his way back to base, all he could mutter to us was, "When I saw the red farmhouse, I turned left; when I saw the four trees, I turned left; but when I looked for the wheat field, it was gone!" It probably never dawned on the pilot that we were in the middle of harvest time and the grain had just been cut.

RAF

On-Call 24 Hours a Day

I joined the RCAF in March of '39 and when the war started, a few months later, I was part of the British Commonwealth Air Training Plan.

We had very little in the way of equipment at first, but that soon improved. We only had something like 4,000 people in the plan in the first year, but by the time the war ended that number had jumped to around 400,000.

Being a machinist by trade wasn't much help to me because they weren't looking for machinists. But they were looking for aero-engine mechanics which I soon became; I had the qualifications because of my four years in auxiliary training prior to the war.

I spent most of my war years—three years—at No. 1 SFTS in Borden, Ontario. Other years were spent at Souris, Manitoba; Torbay, Newfoundland; Brantford, Ontario and others. I instructed most of the time—electrical, engine, air frame—and also did aircraft maintenance.

I remember one time at Borden when a Tiger Moth came in. We didn't want to let him go again because the wind was gusting to around 60 miles an hour but he said he had to get back to Trenton. We walked him out to the runway—there were eight of us, four on each wing—and turned him against the wind. The pilot just opened it up and went straight back about 40 feet! Then as soon as he got up to a 1,000 feet, he justed turned it around and . . . . ZOOOM, he was GONE!! Out of sight. Of course, he had a 60 mile an hour wind behind him.

When he left Borden, we notified Trenton that the pilot was coming. Well, Trenton couldn't understand why we let him go in such a terrible wind. We later heard that when the pilot got there he had to almost fly the Moth right into the ground. Then ground crew had to hold him down or else he'd blow away. You had to take off and land upwind, by the way. Never downwind. When you went upwind you'd get enough pressure under the wings to give you the lift.

You know, I heard that quite a few of the people who went overseas equated anybody who hadn't gone overseas as somebody who didn't want to go over or had the pull to stay home, or they considered us as Zombies, although they never said we were Zombies to our faces. This name-calling, by the way, actually happened after the war. They thought we were having an easy time, but it wasn't so easy for us over here. Many pilots died in crashes and ground crew people worked hard.

We were on-call almost 24 hours a day. All things considered, you sure weren't sitting around doing nothing. The biggest problem was this: when you got an aircraft ready and the pilot took it off the ground you had to be ready when he got back, regardless of the time he got back. Sometimes when people saw us sitting and waiting for the pilots, they thought we were doing nothing. But, you know, we were always busy.

Other times an emergency would come up; like a plane coming in with one wheel up. In most cases the pilot would get the OK to try a belly landing and that's where we came in. You had to get out to the edge of the runway with the equipment in order to lift him off the runway once he stopped. And you had to get him off the runway in a hurry because other planes would have to land, too, or they might run out of fuel while they circled around the base.

Then came the winters. Up to 1940 we never plowed the runways when it snowed because we were using the light pre-war aircraft. During a storm we'd go out and pack down the snow with two or three cats. Once the snow quit then we'd take a couple of hours to pack it down real good. Then we'd get out of the way because some other planes would have to land or take off. Nowadays they use plows all the time.

But once the heavier aircraft came to our stations—the Anson or Harvard, for example—we had to plow. If we didn't and once a thaw came, one of the planes could easily break a wheel off when they landed because, during a thaw, the snow leaves potholes on top of the ashphalt, and this was dangerous to aircraft once the snow froze again.

During my stay with the Air Force you had to consider one fact: you had to enjoy yourself where you hung your hat. If you didn't do that then you wouldn't have any fun or enjoy your stay. As far as my wife and I were concerned, where we hung our hat was home. Simple as that! The accommodations weren't exactly the greatest during the war but you had to live with them. You didn't want to go around being grumpy all the time because you didn't want to make things awful for your fellow workers or your wife.

F/Sgt Joe Lawley
RCAF
2592

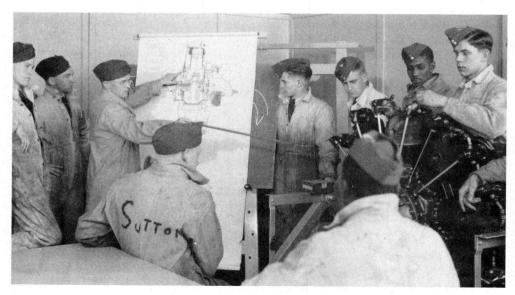

F/Sgt Joe Lawley, at the board, instructing at Camp Borden.

R.C.A.F. FAIREY "BATTLE" (C)

R.C.A.F. FAIREY "BATTLE" (C)

The assembly of a Fairy
Battle at Camp Borden,
Ontario, September, 1939.
      — *Joe Lawley (RCAF)*

23

It was an Emotional and Moving Experience

I remember No. 16 SFTS at Hagersville. July '41. It was the first Wings Parade for the graduating bomber pilots who did their training on Ansons. The place was packed.

During the show the planes were landing and taking off. If one plane got too close to another then one plane would just circle again to avoid a collision. The Ansons had blind spots where a pilot couldn't see straight up or straight down. And there was no radio communication either. The tower would fire up a flare if two planes got too close.

Anyway, two different planes came in for perfect landings, but the trouble was they were both at the same time. At about 50 feet off the ground one Anson landed on top of the other, literally driving the bottom Anson right into the ground and resulting in a big explosion! Right in front of all those people. The women were fainting and guys felt sick to their stomachs. It was awful. The pilot on the bottom was killed while the one on top survived but was injured quite badly.

Later on the same year, only a few days after the Japanese hit Pearl Harbor, an American brigadier general—one star, I think—came up to our base to recruit the American pilots. By the way, I don't think I mentioned that about one-quarter of the pilots were Americans. In fact, one fellow was Phillip Holmes—now I don't know this for sure, but I'm pretty sure it was him—and at that time he was a well-known Hollywood actor.

I can still picture him. what a charmer! He was so handsome he made you sick. He was a great basketball player, too and he used to drive around in a maroon convertible. Not too many pilots had their own transportation back then, but he did. Mind you, he was in his 30's which made him quite a few years older than the rest of us.

Anyway, the brigadier general had all the airmen face him, and he called out for all Americans wanting to transfer to the United States Air Force to take one step forward. Just like the movies. And about half of them stepped forward. It was an emotional and moving experience. The general marched them off and that was it. They were gone.

LAC Bert Nelson
RCAF
R103371

An Avro Anson in flight

FERRY COMMAND

—flying the Canadian and US-built bombers overseas

600 Dollars a Month

In 1939, I was attending the Radio College of Canada in Toronto, taking a training course in commercial radio-operating. When the war broke out in late 1939 I remained at school and graduated in 1940 with a second class commercial-operator's license.

On my way through Montreal, I contacted a good friend of mine who had attended the same radio course. His name was Buck Collins and he had joined the RAF Ferry Command to fly bombers to Britain. When he informed me that they were paying $600 a month for experienced radio-ops, I immediately unholstered my shiny new commercial operator's certificate and made plans to apply for one of these lucrative jobs.

At this early stage the ferrying was being run by the CPR under contract to the British Air Ministry. Shortly after I joined CPR Air Service it changed its name to ATFERO (Atlantic Ferry Organization). Very shortly after that, RAF Ferry Command became the official title.

There were several drawbacks apparent when compared to joining the armed forces. We had no medical coverage or after-the-war benefits. You were on your own. If, by reason of illness you were unable to fulfill your duties, the company could stop your salary for the duration of unavailability. So, the answer was simple: keep healthy, available and keep on enjoying $600 a month.

Because of the shortage of aircraft during the early war years, Ferry Command personnel occasionally found themselves with a lot of spare time on their hands. I personally overcame this problem by spending most of the winter of 1941-42 skiing in the Laurentians.

After the attack on Pearl Harbor and the United States entered the war full time, the aircraft began to flow in ever-increasing numbers and our days of leisure were over. Lockheed Hudsons, Venturas, B-25 Mitchells, B-17 Flying Fortresses, B-24 Liberators and a host of other types began making their appearance on the Dorval Airport tarmac.

In the beginning the usual route was from Montreal to Gander, Newfoundland, then directly across to Prestwick, Scotland. This across-the-North Atlantic-leg of the journey usually took from 10 to 12 hours. The smaller types of aircraft, such as the Hudsons and B-25 Mitchells, did not have sufficient range to cover this distance without the addition of extra gas tanks, usually installed in the bomb-bays and cabins. The 'heavies', like the B-17 or the B-24's, could in some cases make it without auxiliary tanks.

The Consolidated PBY flying boats with the addition of cabin tanks could manage the long trek from Bermuda to Scotland, a distance of about 3,400 miles, nonstop. These Catalina trips were long and tedious, usually of 24-hours duration. You took off from Bermuda early in the morning, flew all day, all night and hopefully landed in Scotland sometime the following morning. I developed a great respect for those rugged old flying boats. I always thought of the tortoise and the hare: so very slow but, oh, so sure!

As the war progressed, the Montreal-to-Prestwick route became a small part of the overall scheme. Planes of every type were ferried to all corners of the earth by a team of civilians in support of the Royal Air Force. The RAF Transport Command, No. 45 Group as it became known in 1943, was comprised of civilians of almost every nationality, together with military pilots from the RAF, RCAF, Free French Air Force, Polish and Norwegian Air Forces; a real 'pot-pourri'.

The early ferrying trips were in some cases hair-raising and in some cases quite uneventful. I guess most of us experienced a little of both. Remember, in those days flying the North Atlantic was still an adventure and not the routine event it is today. We had limited weather information and almost no hope of being rescued after a mid-ocean ditching. You might say you paid your money and took your chances!

I guess I experienced the normal anxieties on my first flight. By the time we arrived at Gander I had convinced myself it was a lost cause. This little twin-engined Lockheed Hudson had no right to try and span 2,100 miles of tossing ocean. But, much to my surprise, 12 hours and 20 minutes later we broke out over Ireland with its green fields and lovely countryside. It is difficult to describe the feeling of exhilaration one experiences when you realize that you are once again over dry land and that terrible premonition you had the night before is now an almost forgotten nightmare. As you start your final descent to the Prestwick runway, your main thought is, "We did it, we did it!" After my second trip, a month later, I began to feel like an old veteran. From then on each trip began to build my confidence until I convinced myself that ferrying was reasonably safe.

Although my first few trips were with rookie crews, I did manage to latch onto a Free French veteran pilot named Jean Mouligne, who was a crack flying-boat man. He was a stable, serious flyer who, to coin an expression, didn't want to be the best pilot in the world; he just wanted to be the oldest. I believe you could say he is probably one of the main reasons I survived the war years.

The Catalina Flying Boat

We made many trips together in all types of aircraft—Catalinas, B-24's, Dakotas, B-25's, Martin Mariners and others. Our trips varied from the 10-hour Gander to UK-flights, to the long but very enjoyable milk runs—Elizabeth City, North Carolina, to Bermuda, Trinidad, Brazil, across the South Atlantic to Africa, up the coast to Gibralter, and the final leg to England. Sometimes a total of 80 hours flying time to reach a destination which, had it not been for the winter weather, could have been accomplished quite easily in a couple of ten-hour hops. You see,

26

it is very difficult to land and take-off on a frozen lake with a flying boat. Of course, the land planes were not afflicted with this problem and could operate throughout the winter months in a normal manner.

I recall one particular B-25 Mitchell delivery which started out in a normal manner in Montreal in July of 1942. I was flying with a young American pilot at the time, named Ken. The plane, serial No. FL 173, a number which has remained in my memory for 40 years, was scheduled for delivery to Britain via Gander.

On the way to Gander, on the first leg of our journey, Ken suddenly decided to land at Moncton, New Brunswick because he knew a girl there. This was not a recommended stop but Ken just said, "We'll say the port engine began to act up and we had to set her down."

So, down we went and left instructions with the ground crew to check over the suspected engine. I think the local crew-chief knew what was up when Ken said we were going into town for the night, but he didn't say anything.

When we checked in at the local hotel, lo and behold Ken seemed to know the hotel receptionist, a rather pretty young thing. Apparently he had met her on a previous trip and it became quite obvious that she was the reason for our unscheduled stop at Moncton. So Ken sent me off to see a movie while he retired to our room with his female companion.

The following morning we went out to the airport and told the crew-chief that we would like to take the plane up for a little test-hop before continuing on to Gander. I kind of think Ken was hoping he could find some legitimate excuse for spending another night in Moncton.

Things being a little slow at the time, the Air Force chap in charge asked if he and a couple of other lads could go up for a quick flight in the B-25, as this plane was relatively new to them. Ken said, "Sure, pile in."

Shortly afterwards, as we are barreling down the runway for take-off, Ken looked over at me and said, "Boy, she's sluggish and mighty tail-heavy compared to yesterday. I wonder what they've done to her?"

Anyway, we took off. We climbed up to about 4,000 feet, circled over Moncton and then came in for a smooth landing. Ken still looked a little perplexed as we were taxiing back to the hangar. He said that the plane seemed too light in the front end.

After shutting down the engines we climbed out of the front exit and watched in horror as body after body descended from the rear hatch. I think we counted about 15 or 16 young RCAF types who had seized the opportunity to stow away and see Moncton from the air. Ken gave them a good-natured lecture on the dangers of wrongly loading an aircraft in this manner, but with the memory of his recent conquest the night before still fresh in his mind, indicated that nothing would be said to the local Air Force Commander.

Shortly afterwards we were on our way to Gander and landed there about three hours later. Twenty-four hours after that we were fully gassed up for a Trans-Atlantic crossing.

About thirty minutes after the Newfoundland coast had dropped behind us, we ran into a driving rain. And I mean RAIN! When I think of the gallons and gallons of water that must have been absorbed by those two roaring engines during the following 14 hours . . . . But that's getting ahead of myself.

When we were about 3 hours out from Gander, I received a coded message which said, "Return to base, weather unfit in Prestwick."

Ken said, "OK, have the navigator give me a course for Gander." We turned around and started back as ordered.

After about an hour another coded message came, which said, "Continue on course to Prestwick." Ken muttered a few curses and referred to the weatherman's ancestors in no uncertain terms. At any rate a quick check of our gas supply indicated that we were still OK for the trip to Prestwick, barring any mishaps.

We covered another two or three hundred miles when another message came, in plain language this time, no time for messing around with any codes. It stated, "Imperative you return to base. Prestwick closed in with no hope of clearing weather for many hours."

Then Ken really got upset, and the cockpit was almost blue. He shouted, "Those damned fools are going to be the death of us yet!"

Having no alternative, we turned back once more for Gander. The navigator quickly worked out an estimated time of arrival, based on the previous ground speed, and the computed wind velocity. Up to this time we had been out for about six hours in driving rain and navigating only by Dead Reckoning, as the navigator was unable to use 'star shots' due to the heavy overcast.

As we came closer to Newfoundland, the radio signals began to improve and we were able to get several 'fixes' which enabled the navigator to plot our position fairly accurately. This wasn't much comfort as Gander, very shortly, began to relay weather messages, indicating a very undesirable situation—200-foot ceiling, visibility one-quarter mile with fog patches.

As we fought our way back, mile by mile and the gas gauges getting lower and lower, things didn't look too bright. Finally, we ended up over the Gander Airport some 13 hours after we had departed. A Radio Range Approach seemed in order, so we went through the procedure, passed over the 'cone of silence' and proceeded to let down at the required rate of descent hoping to line up with one of the runways, and break out in the clear.

This was not to be, however, as the fog by this time was almost on the ground. Ken wisely pulled up and had me contact the control-tower for further instructions. They said, "Stand by for a moment."

About a minute later a voice came on and instructed us to climb to 3,000 feet, fly back over the field and abandon the ship. At this point Ken said, "I'm a pilot, not a bloody parachutist!"

Then he suddenly turned to me and said, "When we flew over Stephenville on our way from Moncton, didn't we see them working on a runway?" He instructed me to get the Stephenville weather conditions and contact the US Army post stationed there that we were on our way. After all, nothing could be worse than Gander with its 'ceiling zero' conditions.

A few minutes later Gander came back with a report saying that Stephenville had a 1,500-foot ceiling with broken cloud and a visibility of one mile. Compared to the Gander weather this was a very acceptable arrangement.

We pumped ever available gallon of fuel from our bomb-bay into the wing tanks and after careful reckoning decided that we might just make it. In the meantime Gander Control had

A Flying Fortress being parked

advised us that although the runway at Stephenville was only partially completed, there should be a stretch long enough to manage a safe landing and that the personnel there would be busy putting out flares to mark the landing strip, as this airport was in the early stages of construction and the runway lighting had not yet been installed.

Sure enough, about one hour later we spotted the partially lit airfield. What an encouraging sight it was, after 14 hours or so of driving rain, lousy weather forecasts and bungled instructions. I contacted the temporary control-tower on the appropriate frequency and told them we were coming straight in, as we were almost out of gas and didn't dare circle the field.

Ken made a beautiful landing on the rain-swept runway. A little jeep appeared in front of us sporting a large "Follow Me" sign attached to its rear. We started back along the runway on our way to the partially built hangar when a few hundred yards short of our destination one of the engines burped a few times then quit. A few seconds later the other engine quit, too. Out of gas, Can you believe it!

A little tractor soon appeared and towed us in. One of the American service personnel, in typical Yankee humor looked at us and said, "Cutting it kind of fine, aren't you fellows." After the last 14 hours of anxiety, this remark served to break the tension and we all enjoyed a good laugh.

The following day was spent waiting for the weather to clear so that we could continue on our journey. The Americans treated us royally during our stay, gassed us up and waved a cheery good-bye as we took off again. One hour later we landed at Gander, collected our codes, topped up the tanks and took-off again for Prestwick. This time the weather was ideal, and ten hours later we set down at Prestwick.

R/O George M. White
RAF/FC
2444

A Trans-Atlantic Record

I navigated on many trips with RAF Transport Command, as it was called when I joined, flying American and Canadian-built bombers to the UK. Our Canadian office was located at Dorval, Quebec, just outside Montreal, and we had another office at Nassau, in the Bahamas. The overseas offices were located in Rabat, Morocco; Karachi, India; Cairo, Egypt, to cover the Middle East; and Prestwick, Scotland, in the United Kingdom—the last stop.

I can recall a few trips for you and at the same time show you the contrast in them.

On one trip, this being in February of '44, we took the train from Montreal to London, Ontario, to fly a Mosquito after it had been test-flown at a London base. We were supposed to take the Southern route over the Atlantic to avoid the winter-ice problems that many pilots faced by going the Northern way. So we started from London and here were the stopovers: Nassau, Puerto Rico, Trinidad, British Guiana, Brazil, and then across to a tiny dot on the map called Ascension Island. This was an American refueling station that had ballooned to a population of a few thousand, which was quite different from its pre-war population of about ten people.

From there we crossed Africa at the Gold Coast, and then we went up to Rabat, then to Marseilles, Paris, and finally to Prestwick. The whole trip took thirteen days and 14,000 miles! Of course we had stopovers to rest and eat, but still that's sure a long haul!

Flying the Mosquito was quite an experience. Only two seats: the pilot and radio-navigator. I had to do the radio work, too. All the navigators did. To get aboard, the pilot climbed in first and sat down, then I got in and closed up the hatch which was at my feet. It was a tight squeeze, let me tell you. Our seats were almost in line, with mine slightly behind and the radio equipment was behind his seat. I navigated with the charts resting on my knees. That's all, nothing fancy. And talk about being busy, I never had time to get bored! I should mention that no matter what plane you flew the navigator was busy, not just with Mosquitos. I would make a calculation on where we were, which would take a few minutes, and by the time I was finished, we were 100 miles past that point. So I had to make another calculation, and so on. Always busy.

One trip with a B-25 Mitchell was a real headache; the plane just wouldn't run properly. We left Gander on January 30, 1944, and finally got to Prestwick on March 13, six weeks later! We had all kinds of problems and delays. A few times we waited for parts to come. On another occasion, an engine quit while in flight. On February 23 we were stuck in Goose Bay, Labrador, without having crossed the Atlantic yet! When we finally left Canada we made stops in Greenland and Iceland—never chancing a non-stop Trans Atlantic flight.

Then in March of '45 I navigated on another Mosquito flight, but this one made world-wide headlines! The pilot on the flight was F/O H. C. Graham. We started from London and took 4 hours to fly 1,300 miles to Gander, at 9,000 feet and a ground speed of 330 miles-per-hour. We stopped to refuel, then took off again, put our oxygen masks on, got up to 21,000 feet, to get the advantage of ice-free weather and a tail-wind of 70 knots, and we landed in Scotland exactly 5 hours and 38 minutes later—a world record for Trans-Atlantic crossings! That was an average speed of 387.5 miles-per-hour! Boy, did we get the headlines! It was front page news. A few hours later another Mosquito, this one flown by Capt. J. H. Naz and navigated by F/L G. Paxton, chopped one minute off our time to make another new record! But we got most of the publicity because we were first.

F/O Hank Seidenkranz
RCAF
J30000

F/O H.C. Graham on left with F/O Hank Seidenkranz on right, after record-breaking Trans-Atlantic flight. In the middle is Capt. J.H. Naz, who broke their record by one minute.
—Hank Seidenkranz
(de Havilland of Canada)

B-24 Liberator, which was ferried overseas, on runway at Ferry Command station at Rabat, Morocco.
—Hank Seidenkranz

The Gas Tank was Riding Empty

The most interesting thing about Ferry Command was the different people you'd meet. They were from all over. One trip you'd go with a guy wearing a cowboy hat and high-heeled boots. These pilots were bush pilots, airline pilots or crop-dusting guys. And we were all in civilian clothes, at least in the first few years. The radio-operators were usually from the Merchant Marine, the Department of Transport, or Marine radio stations.

Most of the trips were far from boring because there was always lots to do while in the air. But when we flew Catalinas, then it was boring. These trips—from Bermuda to Scotland, non-stop—lasted about 30 hours. You'd take off from Bermuda early in the morning and fly all day. Sometime at night you'd only be off the coast of Newfoundland because we had to fly the 'Great Circle Route'. Then we'd turn east for the final leg. We'd land in Scotland in the morning. The Catalinas could only fly at about 90 knots, so you can see why I said these trips were boring.

Once we got to the big planes, like the B-17's and the B-24's, we could climb above the bad weather which the Catalina couldn't do. Other planes we flew were Hudsons, Bostons, DC-3's, Lancasters and many more.

Another way we went was the Australian route where we ferried mostly B-25 Mitchells. Our stopovers were San Francisco, Hawaii, Christmas Island, Canton Island, the Fijis, then Australia.

When it comes to strange experiences, I can remember my third Ferry Command trip. The first two were quite normal. But on the third trip there were about twenty of us leaving Gander right in the middle of a bad front. A couple of the planes had to land in southern Ireland. But when one of them took off they hit a mountain and all the crew died. Two more landed on the beaches over there. Our plane made a wheels-up landing in a hay field just outside Limavady. Hay and cows were flying in every direction, but we came out in one piece.

Another trip, this one with a real great pilot from the USA named Merle Phoenix and the co-pilot, named Tom Bante, another American, was quite unusual.

We were flying a Hudson from Goose Bay, Labrador, and we couldn't see a thing due to the cloud cover and ice. We were somewhere over Greenland, and Merle had the plane on

The twin-engined B-25 Mitchell

automatic-pilot. All of a sudden the Hudson went into a real tight spiral and by the time we came out of it we were in a pocket just over a valley. The cloud was still around us, so we couldn't see above the valley floor. Right away Merle took the plane up as we didn't know where the mountains were. We had no alternative but to take our chances and hope we'd miss the mountains.

We got through the overcast all right, but our DF antenna was bent flat from the excess speed we were travelling in our spiral. We couldn't get any bearings with the DF, so we had to get other radio bearings from Iceland. We circled around for a while until we got the proper bearings and then we flew for Iceland. By now we were very short on gas. Merle said, "Let's get our parachutes on, and the first ship we see, let's get out of here!" But just when he said that, we spotted Iceland. The gas tank was riding empty. There was no time to circle. We flew straight in and landed, and ran out of gas before we reached the end of the runway!

R/O Ron Snow
RAF/FC

Ron Snow in Buenos Aires
two years after the war.

A Quebec Burial

Having enlisted at age 18, I received training as a pilot and upon graduation was posted to Ferry Command shortly after my 19th birthday. The RAF Ferry Command was headquartered at Dorval, Quebec, and had its birth during the height of the war in Europe. Its main function was to arrange for delivery of bombers from North America to Europe, Africa and the Middle East.

In December, 1943, after one flight as a co-pilot in a C-47 (Dakota) to Rabat-Sale, Africa, I was given a 3-month 'Captain's Course' at North Bay, Ontario, to provide further training in Trans-Atlantic ferrying. In April I was on my own and started the business of delivering Mitchells, Dakotas, Liberators and Mosquitos to various parts of the globe.

I had delivered my fourth Mosquito to Prestwick, Scotland in late June, 1945 and had only just returned to Dorval in the morning when I received a phone call from Dodds, our operations officer. He wanted me to catch the train to London, Ontario that night and pick up another Mosquito for ferrying to Scotland.

I had had a pretty busy schedule of flights since completing my 6-hour Mosquito training — 3 hours dual, 3 hours solo — in March, 1945 in Nassau. Maybe I was run down and that made my headcold seem worse than it was. Anyway, Dodds said I would need to get a certificate from the medical officer to delay my trip. He said he was quite short of pilots but would look around to try and find a replacement for me.

I was just leaving the medical officer, having received my certificate of reprieve, when I happened to bump into Sidney Witherspoon, an RAF lad. I briefly told him my story and, of course, he jumped at the chance of a flight as being a married man with a wife in the UK, he could visit his family between trips. He was off to see Dodds and a short time later was on his way.

Montreal was a great city for an officer-pilot during the war. The commissioned ranks in Ferry Command lived in apartments, hotels or what-have-you in the downtown section where the action was. In the mid-forties there was plenty of action to your taste in this metropolitan centre. Being only 20 and with this environment, I gladdened at the opportunity of a night-on-the-town before another trip.

On June 30, I picked up my Mosquito at London, Ontario and headed for Goose Bay, Labrador via Dorval and Mont-Joli. My radio-navigator, Johnny Hardy, was a druggist from London, England.

It was great fun 'shooting up' the boats on the way up the St. Lawrence, but in the Thousand Islands area I developed a malfunction in one of the instruments and thought it was advisable to land at Dorval for repairs.

The ground crew were very understanding when I asked them not to hurry the repairs, and they managed to delay my stopover until 3 PM. With that accomplished, I was delayed overnight in Montreal and again headed for the bright lights.

Next morning, just before take-off, I phoned Frances to tell her I would be 'shooting up' the mountain before heading on to Goose Bay. It was a beautiful and clear Sunday morning as I was circling the mountain and I could see the strollers enjoying the lawns and scenery of this parkland area of Montreal.

Without introduction, the control-tower came in with a curt radio message to immediately return to base. You can imagine my consternation at such an order. The two 1,750 horsepower Packard-Merlin motors created quite a row by alternating the propeller pitch, and my first reaction was, "they have me for low flying."

A request for information on why I must return brought no results. I had a full load of fuel and technically to attempt to land an eleven-ton aircraft with considerable overweight could prove disastrous. Actually, I should have circled to burn fuel for about 2 hours but with curiosity getting the best of me, I decided to go in and land after less than 15 minutes of receiving the return message.

Fortunately, it was one of my best power-approach landings and all I could think of was, "This is it!" I could see the Commanding Officer verbally reducing me to the point where I'd be looking up at the carpet on his office floor.

My reason for recall was because my alternative airport—Mont-Joli—had been rendered unserviceable due to an aircraft accident. With considerable relief I dismissed the 'no details' incident and again made plans to further enjoy Montreal.

Next day, after landing at Mont-Joli, I was told the details of the accident. It was Witherspoon! Apparently he had lost an engine on take-off and stalled on his final approach in his attempt to land on one engine. Mosquitos flew beautifully on one motor but it could be a dicey situation at low altitude, coupled with low speed, lowering undercarriage and flaps in a landing attempt. A circuit away from the dead motor was also not recommended.

The public relations officer had arrived by this time and burial plans were pretty well complete. The other crew member—a commissioned Canadian radio-navigator—was originally from Western Canada and his remains had been sent to relatives for burial.

The business now at hand was to give Witherspoon a proper military funeral with the resources available. There were only two other Mosquito crews besides Hardy and myself, along with half a dozen civilian ground crew around. The Bomber and Gunnery School had departed Mont-Joli some months earlier and the station was now just a staging route for Ferry Command. Finding a Protestant cemetery and an appropriate 'member of the cloth' was also no easy task in the heart of rural Quebec.

We were a sad looking lot as we marched through the downtown streets of Mont-Joli that morning, July 3, 1945. The local residents stared in curiosity at this motley military group following the flag-draped casket. Some of us had only battle dress and I was garbed in khakis. Far cry from the 'dress blues' as protocol called for.

It was a short ceremony at this little graveyard overlooking the St. Lawrence. The Anglican minister we had located administered the last rites in an appropriate and dignified fashion. The tall grass and weeds we all helped to tramp down around the grave provided a better picture for the public relations officer. The widow would receive a photo in due course and through the proper channels. We wanted it to look right. In turn, we each saluted and left.

F/O Walter O. Jones
RCAF
J38997

Jones' B-25 Mitchell approaching Greenland in either 1944 or 1945.

Delivery to India, taken at Rabat-Sale, 1944.
—Walter O. Jones

F/O Jones' Mosquito taken from other Mosquito leaving London, Ont, June 30, 1945.

Walter Jones in middle, with his radio-navigator, Johnny Hardy, on the left and member from other escorting Mosquito. Mont-Joli, Quebec, 1945.

Lockheed Hudsons

COASTAL COMMAND
—protecting the Allied shorelines

Trigger-Happy Gunners

I'll call this first story the 'Lucky landing at Wick'. I was with 269 Coastal Command Squadron and our base was at Wick, Scotland. One of our duties was to patrol the North Sea, taking care of our sector in case the Germans ever attempted an invasion. We'd go out with our twin-engined Hudsons as far as the coast of Norway, then come back—a dawn-to-dusk patrol.

One time we came back at night and we were all very tired. I was the 'second-dickey' on that trip—the second pilot. Now, our aerodrome had no runways, just an open field which had a nice long stretch running east and west. The only other alternative was much shorter, running north and south, but the snag with that route was the last, roughly, one-third of the distance was downhill in the north-south direction. The aerodrome control were given strict instructions to lay the flare path east-west, and only use north-south if the wind was blowing more than 20 miles-per-hour cross the field.

We saw the flare path running southerly, down the hill, but we didn't give it much thought. We touched down fairly close to the beginning of the field, applied the brakes and the Hudson slowed down. We gave it 'full flap' and it slowed down some more. Then we really reemed on the brakes as hard as we could! Now the wheels were locked and we were skidding! Well, we ran smack into a blastproof shelter! These were the shelters used to protect a plane from enemy bombs. It was an 8-foot high, U-shaped wall that the plane was pushed into to protect it from any bomb blasts. We hit the shelter with the nose of the aircraft riding up the ramp and we pushed the port engine back; and the only gas we had was in the port wing. The oil line, lucky for us, didn't go but I do remember seeing the white fumes from the gas hitting the hot exhaust. If the oil line had broken we would've been in flames. We had a lucky landing that time.

A little while after that accident we were fired on by a British anti-aircraft cruiser while we were escorting a convoy approaching the Pentland Firth; the channel between the north shore of Scotland and the Orkney Islands. The convoy was in a close-square formation and would have to squeeze down to pass through the channel.

We were told of the cruiser's position near the convoy during the pre-flight briefing and also given the 'letter of the day'. When approaching any surface craft we always signalled them that letter to identify ourselves as being friendly and received a reply. The signal was usually sent by Aldis lamp which was pointed at the vessel and the Morse letter was flashed with a trigger switch.

When we arrived at the scene at almost 2,000 feet, the cruiser was quite near the convoy. We sent our signal. We patrolled around the convoy and repeated the signal procedure each time we went near the cruiser. After doing this at least six times, I told my second-dickey not to bother any more, as I knew we were within sight of the ship during the entire trip around the convoy and the weather was excellent. As I flew near the ship, I was looking down at it when I saw the flash and smoke of gunfire. Then I looked out to sea to watch the shells splash into the water. I then saw explosions ahead and dead in line with our flight path. We could smell the smoke when we flew through it.

I turned away and took the craft down to sea level and told the second-dickey to call the cruiser, by lamp, and ask why the heck they fired at us.

Word came back saying, "We were firing at your towed sleeve."

They tried to claim we were carrying a target sleeve, the ones that air-gunners used to practice on. The sleeves were towed by the aircraft with a long wire and the gunners would shoot at it. Sometime after this our squadron got an apology from the Navy. I guess some trigger-happy gunner went a little wild.

You know, I just have to mention what I saw in June of 1940 when I was stationed on the island of Guernsey; one of the British-owned islands close to the French shore. This was just a few days after the fall of France. I don't know for sure how many people saw it but I know myself and at least three others witnessed it.

We saw the French Air Force, in strength, about 5 miles in the distance flying out towards safety in England. They were at all heights. There were bombers, fighters, light aircraft, biplanes, monoplanes; all kinds. I don't know how many aircraft were involved but I'd say, conservatively, about 200. We clapped and cheered because we were so happy for them! Then, to our amazement, they turned around and flew back to France! We were horrified! That's what they did and I've never seen that in print anywhere. But I know it happened because we saw it. The pilots and crew were probably told that their families would suffer if they didn't return. The word must've come when they were in the air.

RAF

Hunting Subs off the coast

The Canadian Coastal Command was no picnic, not even for us mechanics. They worked us like dogs; we'd get only a 48-hour pass every three weeks. I worked on all kinds of planes—Mosquitos, Liberators, Lysanders, Catalinas, Cansos, Dakotas, Lancasters, Hudsons, Hurricanes and a few others.

When the war started I was 32 years old and I wanted to be a pilot with the RCAF, despite my age. But the pilot age-limit was 26. I was told by the RCAF to just hang on because they'd raise the age, and that I should take an engineer's course while I was waiting. A couple years later they raised the age-limit to 28, but by that time I was 34, so I gave up on that idea and became a mechanic instead. I qualified because I had finished the course, third highest in the class.

I spent the summer of '41 in North Sydney, Nova Scotia where we flew the Stranraer; a British bi-plane which was quite a sound aircraft. Then I was posted to Dartmouth where I spent the winter of '41 and '42. There we did coastal duty while flying the Catalina flying boat, and the Canso (a Catalina with wheels). They were some planes! The crew consisted of a pilot, co-pilot, navigator, radio-operator, two aero-engine mechanics and one aero-frame mechanic, which I was, although I could do both mechanic jobs. Then we'd add three gunners if we were out on sub duty. We cooked, ate and slept on there. The Catalina could carry over 1,400 imperial gallons of gas in its wings and another 700 gallons in auxiliary tanks and could stay in the air for many, many hours; sometimes a day or more.

Do you remember the Churchill-Roosevelt conference aboard a ship just off the Newfoundland coast? Well, I was there: Placentia Bay in August of '41. We were up at 15,000 feet and circling to provide cover (from five in the morning till eleven at night with one stop to refuel). Below us were other boats—an aircraft-carrier in particular—and just above them were fighter planes flying back and forth and circling. If one of Hitler's subs were going to attack they'd sure get it. Security was tight that day.

You know, our crew found some subs, too, but that kind of stuff never reached the papers. The Government didn't want Canadians to know that German subs were only a few miles off our coastline. Heck, one sub got one of our boats just outside the Halifax harbour. They cut it right in two!

On one of our searches I spotted, from my blister, a sub on the beach of Sand Isle—an island just a few miles from Dartmouth. As we flew by the sub we noticed it wasn't moving. We immediately guessed it had gone aground. So we contacted our tower and found out later that there were no Germans aboard; they had taken off! A day or so later a few government boys from

Ottawa came down to have a look at the captured sub. We heard later that a couple of Germans were found in Halifax with theatre tickets in their pockets, so we put two and two together.

Hunting subs was like this: if we spotted one we'd get down closer and drop a couple depth charges, the Catalinas carried four under their wings, on both sides of the sub and we'd have them set to go off at about 30 feet. And then . . . . BOOM! We'd get them. One time we cut a sub right in half and the water was gushing straight out the top of it!

One time on a Stranraer, we were about 300 miles off the coast when an American ship started shooting at us. They probably didn't recognize the plane and thought that if it wasn't one of theirs then it had to be a German. What a German plane would be doing 300 miles off the Canadian coast, I don't know, but that's probably the way they thought. One of the bullets cut a tail strut as I was walking down the fuselage and the force of it caused me to fall down and I cut my ear quite badly. It swelled up so bad that when I got back to shore I saw a doctor. Oh, did it look awful! Just like a cauliflower ear. So the doctor drained the fluid. Heck, I didn't want any cauliflower ear the rest of my life.

Sgt Joe Nadeau
RCAF
R84211

A Desert Rainstorm

The year was 1944. We took off from England in a B-24 Liberator and arrived at Rabat in West Africa. We stopped there for a couple of days before we went right across North Africa to Cairo. That was a long distance back then, about 2,000 miles, and the aircraft in those days didn't carry too much fuel.

Just outside Cairo we ended up getting caught right in the middle of a darn sandstorm and we couldn't even see the ground. We were talking to the base, but we couldn't see them. They were saying to us, "We can hear you. Fly around and we'll talk you down to the runway."

We kept flying around but we still couldn't see anything. By now things were getting a little hectic because we were running out of fuel and we had to land somewhere. We were even thinking of landing on a road if we could find one. We somehow picked out a road, but just then we also spotted a runway right in front of us. So down we went and landed. The trouble was we landed at the wrong airport, which happened quite a bit in that area. We landed at an American base, not the RAF base that we were supposed to land at.

These two airports were so close to each other, maybe 5 or 10 miles apart, that you could talk to one airport and land at the other, which was exactly what we did.

Anyway, we spent the night there. In the morning the dust settled. We got on the plane, took off, got up about 100 feet, then landed at the RAF base.

When we got to the RAF base, they put us under canvas. Now, we all know it doesn't rain in the desert all that often. Well, let me tell you, it sure rained that night! The tent collapsed from the rain, and what a mess! Back then you didn't have these nice nylon tents like you have today. We had the heavy canvas ones, and everything just collapsed from the weight. My bag was buried in the sand from the force of the rain.

The next morning the sun was shining and everybody took off into town. Everybody except me. I hauled the stuff out of the tent and hung up my clothes to dry in the sunshine. I got pictures of the whole thing.

When we got to Karachi, India a couple days later, they put us under canvas again. We hung around Karachi for a while with nothing spectacular happening. From there we got posted to 200 Squadron of Coastal Command, just south of Madras, at a place called St. Thomas Mount. This was an RAF outfit.

I remember, too, the rope beds we used to sleep on. They were just a 2x4 frame with four legs, roped vertically and horizontally, and a mattress about an inch thick and filled with straw. We also had a mosquito net around the bed. Every morning we had to check our boots for snakes or scorpions.

F/O Nick Mozel, at front left, with other crew members in front of their B-24 Liberator, India 1944.

F/O Nick Mozel's clothes drying out after dessert rain storm.

I recall one time when this Aussie left and went to his barracks and, all of a sudden, we heard a shot and some yelling. I guess this guy found a snake in his boot, pulled out his revolver and started firing away.

Our job on Coastal Command, I was the co-pilot on our crew, was anti-submarine patrol over the Bay of Bengal, and to escort convoys in the same area.

This one time we were briefed on where this certain convoy was. We picked it up and signaled it with our Aldis lamp. They told us what kind of search to do, where to go and so on, because there were various types of searches. This time we went off, searched around a bit, then were supposed to come back to the convoy, and be told what else to do. Well, when we finished our search and got back, there was no convoy! I didn't know if our radar wasn't working or what, but we couldn't find the ships. We flew around looking for it, but pretty soon the gas was getting low and we had to turn back to base. To this day I don't know where the convoy went!

We flew the Liberator while on patrols. It was a fine aircraft. I remember we used to do drills on ditching because all of our operational flying was done over water. To do this we had regular drills on the ground. The Liberator was an excellent aircraft but it wasn't till long after the war was over that I found out there was only one successful ditching of a Liberator. Because of the way they were built, 999 times out of 1,000 they would snap in two once they hit the water and sink almost instantly. There was only one pilot that I know of who made a successful ditching of a Liberator, and it stayed afloat for 20 minutes. I'm glad we never had to ditch one because our chances were about nil.

Because we did a lot of night flying, our Lib was fitted with a huge, powerful light under the wing. Also, we had a generator aboard to produce the electricity for this light. The theory behind the night patrols was this: we'd fly around till we picked up something on our radar. From there we had a certain pattern to fly. The radar-operator would tell us how to fly and how low to get. After we successfully flew the pattern and we were about a mile away, the radar-operator would say, "Now!" Then we'd switch the light on the target. Submarines would come up at night to recharge their batteries and this was the time we were supposed to go after them, drop some depth charges, then get out as soon as we could. The light did serve a useful purpose.

Besides submarines, there were a lot of British Navy ships around, but we were usually briefed on where they were. The Navy was notorious for 'shooting first and asking questions later.'

There was one time I fired at my own Liberator. We were on patrol when I left my seat and went back to one of the .50-calibre beam guns, which could swing out on both sides. I opened the window, swung out the gun, loaded it, cocked it and pulled the trigger, but forgot about the recoil. Well, that darn gun swung around and hit me! It was first pointed out the side of the plane, but it swung around and headed for the tail. The gun hit me in the chest, and luckily I let go or else I would have shot my own tail off. When you swung the gun out there was a big pin used to lock the gun to the side of the aircraft, and I didn't do it. I just loaded and fired. That was the closest I ever came to shooting my own aircraft down.

F/O Nick Mozel
RCAF
J37984

Just The Man We Need

My job on the base at Prince Rupert, B.C. consisted of checking aircraft instruments—altimeters, fuel-pressure gauges, verticals, horizons, wind velocity—on the ground with testing equipment hooked up to them, and in the air to make sure that they worked properly.

Most of my flying was done on the Stranraer and the Swordfish. Flying in the Stranraer was quite an experience because its two wings—it was a bi-plane—would flap just like a bird. The Swordfish, another bi-plane, was a better plane. It carried torpedoes and had a crew of two—pilot and gunner.

To inspect the planes when they were in the bay, two of us had to row out to them. Once we got in, we'd look the instruments over, test the switches and so on.

One time, some guys went out to inspect a plane but one guy pulled a wrong switch — the one for the depth charges — and . . . . BAM!!! The plane was blown right out of the water. Once the water-spray and debris cleared we saw one fellow hanging on the tail section while the other fellow disappeared completely! Gone! We finally found him a few days later at the bottom of the bay in 80 feet of water.

I actually tried to get into the RCAF as a cabinet-maker and carpenter but I was told at the recruiting station that they didn't need them. They advised me to try a course in instrument mechanics, instead. When I was sent to Trenton to take the course, they said to me, "Sorry, we don't need any instrument-mechanics. What else can you do?"

"Well, I'm a cabinet-maker and —"

"Just the man we need!" the man interrupts. And that happened at every base I went to.

The strangest episode for me happened back at Prince Rupert. One night something showed up on our radar instruments and we didn't know what it was. Something was out there in the harbour and it must have slipped through the submarine nets. Our first thought; a Japanese sub!! So we grabbed some guns and ran down to the shore and jumped into the trenches, the ones that were always full of water due to constant rain, and waited. If it was a sub and it ever surfaced, then I guess we were supposed to blast it out of the water with our guns. Anyway, we couldn't see a thing. How could we! All we could see was black sky and black water.

The whole area was under alert. There were anti-aircraft guns up on the rocks and behind us. An American base only a few miles away was also ready. So, there we all were: till the next morning, but nothing happened. The whole alert was then called off and nobody told us why.

Finally, sometime in the afternoon we were told. A whale had slipped through the sub nets!

Cpl Eric Bodden
RCAF
R161175

Cpl Eric Bodden with testing equipment at RCAF station at Comox, B.C., Feb. 1945.

RCAF base at Comox, BC., Vancouver Island. B-24 Liberator at right.

Comox, BC, RCAF station. Dakota in foreground.

I Never Lost an Airplane

When I was with 404 RCAF Squadron in Scotland, I serviced Beaufighters.

We were part of Coastal Command—anti-shipping. That meant our pilots went after German ships in and around the North Sea and would fire at them with rockets or torpedoes.

The policy when I first joined the 404 was for the mechanics to work on a different plane each day, and I didn't like that at all. So, one day when they told me to go and work on a certain aircraft, I said, "Why should I work on everybody else's plane? Why can't I keep the same one. It's like friendly competition. Each man will know what has to be done on his own aircraft, and he'll be responsible for his own. He'll look after it better."

They agreed to it and shortly after other mechanics started doing the same thing. Pretty soon a plane was getting to be known by its mechanic; a mechanic was getting to be known by his aircraft.

One day, five or six pilots came to our squadron and one of them came up to me while I was working on the wing of my Beaufighter. He climbed the ladder and stepped onto the wing. There I was in my greasy clothes, and there he was in his spanking new uniform.

"Hi, I'm Johnson," he says, "How's this airplane?"

"It's the best," I told him. I meant it, too. It was like bragging about something I had to live up to.

"Well, I heard you never lost an airplane." Almost every mechanic on the squadron had lost at least one plane.

Then he says, "Do you mind if I fly your aircraft?"

And I said, "By all means, you're certainly welcome. Go ahead!" The irony of him asking me was that he was a pilot officer and I was only an LAC.

And I remember some of the other pilots we had. One pilot would always come away with top honours when he went on training exercises where he did gun firing or rocket firing; but he was so short that he needed extra cushions to sit on so he could see the gun sight. That didn't seem to matter because he also had the best shot in combat conditions. I would later see aircraft photos that were taken from planes and put in books or newspapers to show how to properly attack ships. Many of them were his pictures; taken while flying my aircraft!

I never did lose a plane. I spent a lot of time on mine. I made sure I knew it inside out, and I anticipated problems that might come up.

I worked on one particular Beaufighter that put in 300 hours on Coastal Command. I had a certain reputation and my aircraft became, shall we say, invincible. Later on, when we got rockets in the squadron to replace the torpedoes, they used to paint a little rocket on the side of the Beaufighters to show that it had attacked a German ship. Well, I had 43 rockets on the side of my plane before they stopped putting them on. I think my pilots were getting a bit worried because if any German fighter saw all those rockets, then they'd go after my plane right away.

Another pilot I remember really loved to fly, he went on three tours. One time, a large shell went through his wing and damaged the aileron. He flew the plane back about 50 feet off the water which was tough because the aircraft wanted to flip right over, due to the enormous amount of drag put on that wing. He pushed the controls to maximum but the force to hold it there was too much for one man. So the navigator had to crawl from the back part of the plane, over boxes of cannon shells, to get to the cockpit. He grabbed the axe handle from the side of the craft, jammed it into the control column, and these two men, held the plane level all the way back to England. Normally, they should've just taken it up higher and jumped out, but not this pilot. Mind you, I don't know of anyone who successfully jumped out of a Beaufighter, anyway.

My favorite story on the Beaufighters was about a 'scare' gun, a .303, in the back. When it was installed you could swing the gun around but when the tail section got in the way of the barrel, then the gun was supposed to lock. You could shoot up to it and around it without shooting your tail off.

Well, one day our squadron CO went out to test the gun and ended up shooting off his own tail. That poor mechanic sure got it for that one! He was court-marshalled and spent twenty-nine days in what we called the 'glass house'. Then they started checking out all the other planes and found that every other gun could shoot off their own tails!

All this had been going on for more than a year without anybody hitting a tail, at least not that we know of. Mind you, some of the Beaufighters never came back and we didn't know how we lost them. Sometimes the weather was bad, but it couldn't have been bad on all those occasions. So, here was this poor guy who spent twenty-nine days in the 'glass house' because of a bad design, which he had nothing to do with. All this time, everybody just assumed that it would work. Too bad it had to take a year to find out about the whole thing.

Beaufighter Comments

A good solid aircraft. It certainly was not in the same class as a Messerschmitt, as far as being a fighter. It wasn't really maneuverable but it sure had the armament—four cannons and six machine guns. It also had torpedoes and, later, rockets under the wings. It was built solely for hitting ships, which it was highly successful at.

LAC Don Kulik
RCAF
R160120

The Beaufighter

Fairey Battles on the runway at No. 3 Bombing and Gunnery School, Macdonald, Manitoba, 1943.

THE FAR EAST

stories from India, Burma and China

Dropping Supplies

I spent twenty months as a staff-pilot at the Bombing and Gunnery School in Macdonald, Manitoba and in September, 1944 I finally made it overseas. I was sent to England.

In England I trained with a fellow from London, Ontario, as his co-pilot. Then we were posted to an RAF squadron at a base near Oxford, England. We flew to the Continent to bring 'priority wounded' back to England, mostly Army men who were in need of operations.

From there I was posted back for retraining, where I became a captain of my own crew. Then I was sent to southern England for a rather unique course: Glider Pick-up. The training consisted of three weeks where we practised snagging an elevated nylon loop which was attached to the glider.

On VE day, Victory Europe, we were in London and the next day we took off for India.

I made stops in Karachi, Calcutta and Burma and then was posted to 435 RCAF Squadron at Imphal. I reported to the adjutant at Imphal but he had never heard of me. I showed him my papers and he said, "Oh, my God! You should be down with 31 Squadron on Ramree Island."

The Japs at this time were still in Burma, retreating down the Irrawaddy Valley to Rangoon. We did our part by flying troops and supplies from our base at Ramree, over the mountains and onto strips on the other side.

These strips weren't like the regular strips that we were used to back in England. Many of them were dirt, while others were steel-matted or asphalt strips. If you think of asphalt roofing or tarpaper; that's what they put down over the sand. Every once in a while this roofing would peel up from the wind and sometimes blew right in front of you as you were landing.

Our squadron started at 3 in the morning and the last takeoff was about 4 in the afternoon. There weren't any droppings at night except for special missions. The all-up weight on our Dakotas was 31,500 pounds. We hauled things like food, fuel, mail and troops.

I remember one dropping in particular, just to give you an idea of what it was like. We did three droppings on that one trip.

First of all, we got a briefing on Ramree Island before we set out. We flew at low altitude, right down at the water and map-read our way down to Sandoway. We came in over the dropping zone and I let the crew know that we were getting close. Then I rang the bell, which was the crew's signal, and the supplies were pushed out. They were sacks of potatoes, three of them to a parachute. After they were all out we left the area for the next drop which was down the Sandoway River.

On the way down we ran into a pouring rainstorm. Our windshield wipers were going like mad and I remember that we came over this one hill and I could see the drop zone. As we got right over it, I pushed the bell and out went a big waterproof container of mail for the troops below. Our drop point was close to the river, but we missed a little and the container landed right in the water. I circled around and I could see two guys jump into a canoe and paddle like crazy out to the container.

From there we went down to 'straight drop' some medical supplies at about 10 feet off the ground. There were no parachutes involved this time, just right out the door.

According to my log book I put in a total of 342 hours in Burma. A complete tour was 700 hours, so I was a long way off from that. To get in those hours a lot of trips were involved. Some trips would take 2½ hours while others might take only an hour. The strategy was to get in at least 100 hours a month. Some months I flew 150 hours, but that was too hard on you.

F/O B. Rich
RCAF
J47509

31 Squadron members—all Canadians —on Ramree Island. Left to Right: Harold Corey, unidentified, Harry Clarke and F/O Barney Rich.

Through the door of F/O Rich's Dakota, over the Arakan Mts.

The Hooghly Belle

We left Canada and sailed to Gourock, Scotland. From there we took the train to Hastings, England, on the English Channel. When we arrived there, we had about a mile to walk to get to our hotel. We were right at the edge of the front. I remember the Air Force warrant officer telling us, "There will be no stops for resting. You've got to carry your kit bag because Jerry comes across the Channel quite often."

We were billeted in a brand new hotel which had never been put into service. We were on the seventh floor and when we got to the room, all of a sudden, we heard a plane outside. We walked out to the balcony and right at eye level was a German Me-109! He was only about 100 feet away and you could actually see the pilot. He just went past the hotel, banked and went back across the Channel without firing a shot. This was quite an introduction to the war!

I was in England for a while, in Durham County, then posted to Cornwall. Four of us were posted down there to take over a radar station that the British Army had been using for plotting the shipping in the Channel. When the Air Force took it over, we were to plot aircraft activity. We liked it there because we were our own bosses and could come and go as we pleased as long as the work was done. But after a few months of that I applied for further overseas postings, and in about two weeks time I was on my way to India.

We left Liverpool and it took us six weeks to get down to Durban, South Africa. That was a pretty slow convoy. We spent five weeks there before we took another ship to India.

I had a number of postings in the Calcutta area, before I finally got posted to a new radar barge which was being constructed out of an old coal barge. It was the first of its type, a floating radar barge which we called the 'Hooghly Belle'. It had no motor power of its own and had to be towed. The idea behind it was that it would still be mobile enough to move up with the invasion hops and give air-radar cover. Our barge was about 85 feet long by about 16 feet wide. We ate, slept and worked right on it. The living quarters were down below the deck and could carry about twenty people.

Once we were on the barge we went to the Hooghly River then went through the Sundarbans (The Mouths of the Ganges River) where there are hundreds of islands and many waterways. It took about a week to go through there and it was really quite an experience; we could see wild game on some of the islands. This was during the week between Christmas and New Year's and we didn't have any Christmas dinner. But along the way we shot a deer and had fresh venison.

After that we went to Chittagong and then down the coast to Akyab. It was here at Akyab that we were instrumental in the shooting down of our first Japanese aircraft.

We were a GCI radar station—Ground Control Interception. We picked up this aircraft on our screen and it was identified as the enemy. We got the Spitfires to scramble from their station. I forget for sure where the station was. It might've been from an aerodrome at Argartala or from Chittagong. The Spitfires, there were two of them, went all out to catch up with this plane.

The Jap, flying an 'Oscar', had the plane up around 34,000 feet on a reconnaissance mission. The Spits caught up with him and shot him down and the Oscar landed in the sea, just off the coast of Ramree Island which was about 75 miles from our station. There was a radar station on Ramree island, only a few hundred yards away from the crash site, and they didn't know there was a plane overhead. The Oscar was up high enough to be out of range of the radar lobe.

Another experience happened when we were leaving New Year's morning, 1945, to pick up a convoy just outside the port of Chittagong. After picking up the convoy we were supposed to go down the coast of Burma, rendezvous at an island off the coast and then give coverage on aircraft activity. But, just outside the harbour at Chittagong, we could see a couple of naval vessels about a half-mile away and they cut across our bows at a pretty good clip. They threw off some large waves which came towards us and there was nothing we could do. Our barge was top-heavy to begin with, and we thought it would turn over for sure when the waves hit us.

We were just in the process of being hooked up to a corvette when the waves hit and they almost did turn us over. In fact, this was the only time I actually saw rats deserting what they thought was a sinking ship! They jumped off the barge and clung onto the ropes of the corvette. We survived the ordeal but got rid of the rats.

It was on this occasion I was recommended for a decoration. When the waves hit the barge one of our crew was knocked overboard, right between the barge and the corvette and the two were bumping together. I jumped in and grabbed this fellow, who was a non-swimmer. Then we were thrown a life preserver and were pulled into the corvette.

Now it just so happened a senior officer was on our barge at the time and he saw what happened. From there he put words in the right places and I got mentioned in the King's New Year's Honour List of 1946. From this I received the British Empire Medal.

Cpl William B. Kerr
RCAF
R122935

Why Didn't The Japs Fire at Us?

Burma, during the war, was something you didn't want to miss, but you wouldn't want to do it again, either. It was hot and wet there; the Monsoons were especially rough. It could easily rain 5 or 6 inches overnight. Then you had to dig a trench around your tent so the water wouldn't get in.

On the runways were steel mats laid over the mud. But each time we landed the steel mats would sink deeper and deeper into the mud. Then the water would come over top and pretty soon we couldn't land at all.

When the summer came things were completely different: it was dusty and they even tried to water-down the dirt landing strips. But it didn't seem to do any good. One time I saw two fighters come in, one behind each other, and the first one raised so much dust that the second one didn't see the first one and smashed into him, chopping him to pieces.

A Dakota in Burma

I was a WAG, wireless-operator air-gunner, with 436 Squadron; but I did other things, too, like kicking and dropping out supplies to the British Army.

One day we took a load of supplies down to the front. On one hill were the Japanese and on the other, the British. We dropped our supplies in front of the British and took off out of there. All this time I wondered why the Japanese never even fired at us. We must've been a few hundred yards from the Japs and normally they would've taken a few shots at us.

When I got back to base, I asked the liason officer, "Why didn't the Japs fire at us?"

"They didn't fire at you because they were close enough to drive the British back, then take all the supplies for themselves. Of course they didn't want to fire at you; you were supplying them!"

F/O R. W. Eves
RCAF
J4653

Rice in a Double Bag

After spending time training in Canada, I arrived at Bournemouth, England. From there I was sent to an Operational Training Unit in Limavady, Northern Ireland. That was October, 1943.

Northern Ireland in the latter part of the year is a cold, wet, cloudy, damp place and the sun hardly ever shines. We went to school in the morning, when it was still dark, and when we got out sometime in the afternoon, the darkness had set in again. Consequently, we saw very few daylight hours and to add to it, we did most of our flying at night.

From there I went to 415 RCAF Coastal Command Squadron at Bircham Newton on the east coast of England. Our job was to fly up and down the coasts of Germany, Belgium and Holland to look for German ships. We also had to protect our own coastline from German shipping and aircraft.

The first night we went on Coastal Command we flew our Wellington quite low over some German E-Boats; they were like a torpedo boat only much faster and they carried .50-calibre guns. They waited till we flew over a couple times, then they smartened up, formed a circle and let us have it with their machine guns. Fortunately, they missed.

Another time, we had been out flying most of the night and when we got back to base we were told we couldn't land there and that we'd have to land at a place called Thorney Island. At our briefing, before we set out, we were told a brand new radar base was being built at Thorney Island and that it was the most powerful base in all of England. It was just getting the finishing touches on it that night and we were given the new call letters for it.

When we approached Thorney Island, unfortunately, radio communication wasn't exactly the best because they didn't identify us as a Coastal Command aircraft and wouldn't turn the lights on. In the meantime our starboard motor gave out as we approached, the motor that supplies the electricity which operates the radio equipment, so we couldn't contact the base.

With all this in mind, our pilot made a beautiful landing, although a little too fast, and we went off the runway, took out the brand new radar base and wound up in the English Channel, landing on the water flat as a pancake. This was in March, and the water was pretty damn cold! Fortunately, no one was hurt. We landed in shallow water and waded back to shore.

Following our tour of operations in England we were sent to Burma, where they were forming two Canadian transport squadrons—435 and 436—and it was going to be our job to drop supplies to the British 14th Army, who were in the process of pushing the Japs out of India and Burma and back into the ocean. I went to 436.

Strangely enough, back in England, when we were told we were going to be sent to Burma, some of the guys kept saying how warm it was down there. But one of the places we stayed, Chaklala, was up in the foothills of the Himalayan Mountains. When we went to bed at night we put our clothes on and got all the blankets we could find because it was darn cold.

When we arrived in Burma we started our operations in mid-January of 1945. We either

Training ten members of the Gurkha Army in parachute jumping at Chaklala, India. F/L Bill Sims is third from left in front row and beside him is Gene Balbry. Two English officers, in the middle of the back row, also helped in the training, 1944.

The Patkai Range and a bit of wing of the Dakota, over the India-Burma border. They flew over these mountains on the Imphal Valley-to-Shwebo route, 1944.

dropped or landed supplies out of our base at Imphal. Then we flew from there, over the mountains, into a place called Shwebo. It had taken the British something like six months to push the Japs back to Shwebo and we could fly from Imphal to Shwebo in less than an hour. The British had to drive the Japs through jungles so thick that when we flew over you couldn't see anything underneath the trees—no rivers, no land, nothing—until you got to the plains at Shwebo!

I remember one time in Burma we were on the ground waiting for a wounded Beaufighter to come back after he had dropped some bombs. He came back on one engine and, unfortunately, slammed into our Dakota, killing the co-pilot, F/Sgt England.

The weather in Burma was hot, and the only way we could cool off was to fly up high.

The food was another story. In England it was much better, if you liked brussel sprouts twice a day. But in Burma we usually had to survive on K rations which were an assortment of pre-packaged foods, like the famous Spam. Fresh vegetables were very hard to come by.

Burma was an interesting part of the war because the 14th was moving so fast that sometimes we'd drop supplies at a particular point, then two days later pick it up and drop it further, so the Army could get them.

We not only carried supplies. One time we hauled pound notes and sterling to the British Army, so they could get paid. Other times we brought back wounded soldiers. So you might say our Dakotas were a two-way aircraft.

Whenever we landed near the Army we always got a chance to talk to some of the soldiers. You know, no matter how hot it was, they always had a kettle and a pot of tea ready.

I was a wireless operator, air gunner, radar operator and 'kicker outer'. The idea was to kick the supplies out as quickly as you could, then get out of there. Most of the time we were dropping 'free falls', like rice which had a double bag. Some of the other supplies had to be parachuted down. The heavier supplies, oil and gas drums, couldn't be dropped; so we had to land these. We were usually dropping the supplies at about 500 feet, except for the parachuted ones which went out at around 900 feet.

The landing strips were nothing great. They were just dirt. And there was no such thing as landing or taking off into wind. Whatever way the airstrip was, that's the way you went.

We had about twenty aircraft in our squadron, all twin-engined Dakotas, and we tried to keep fifteen serviceable every day. We had two crews per aircraft, and they flew every other day. You took off as close to dawn as you could to get in as many trips as you could—sometimes as many as five—then get back before nightfall because there were no lights at our base. You had to do everything by daylight. By that time, the first part of 1945, the days were longer anyway because it was their summer.

As the Japs were pushed out to the ocean, our base moved from the original site in the Imphal Valley to Akyab, an island on the west coast of Burma. We were never more than an hour away from the lines.

The war in Burma was really something. You wouldn't have wanted to miss it for anything, providing you got back in one piece. But a lot of them didn't come back in one piece, and a lot of them didn't come back at all.

F/L Bill Sims
RCAF
J23643

Terror in a P-51

My one hour flying-time in a P-51 was the 'straw that broke the camel's back' and motivated me to quit flying in the China-Burma-India Theatre in March, 1945.

On January 14, 1943, 3,500 Aviation Cadets received their Army pilot's wings. Being one of these, I was assigned to dive bombers for six months. Then the Army realized that the U.S. Navy could do a better job of manning the dive bombers and sent us Army A-24 pilots to various fighter transition groups.

I went to P-47's and found that the P-47 instructor pilots were almost as afraid of the 'Jug' as we trainee pilots were. We never were allowed or encouraged to 'Split S' the P-47. We were merely allowed to fly two-ship elements, and loosely at that! We did a great deal of 'rat racing' among the beautiful 20,000 foot-high cumulo-nimbus storm clouds. We had some altitude flights. I remember being told how to make a tight turn by pulling up the nose, holding top rudder and pulling the stick back and to the right. This allowed the torque to pull me around in a sort of skid. We were cautioned that the fuselage was blocking out the air flow and that there was danger in flopping 'over the wing.'

I did not care for the P-47, and at the first sign of knee trouble I reported to dispensary with a 'trick knee'. I was duly grounded, transferred to a general hospital and then, after the knee healed, shipped out to P-40's. This was a good ship and I went to the CBI Theatre as a fighter pilot along with two dozen other 'P-shooters'.

The P-40 Tomahawk

Upon arrival in India, in January '44, we fighter boys learned that a dozen of us were to become C-47 transport co-pilots. All of us applied ourselves and after a couple of hundred co-pilot hours, we took over as first-pilots. We competed against each other to see how fast we could become captains.

After 800 hours of mashing the C-47 controls and throttles around over the Hump, in the Hump, and around the Hump, I found myself landing at Kunming, the home of the Flying Tigers. An old-time buddy and fighter-pilot who was Assistant-Operations Officer spotted me climbing out of a C-47 one day and said, "Ralph, you have to check out a P-51 before this old war is over. Do it now," he urged.

"OK," I said, a little fearfully.

He brought me over to the Mustang, showed me how to start it up, closed the canopy, jumped off the wing and motioned me away. I cleared with the tower, taxied to the take-off position, checked the mags, lined up with the runway and 'poured the coal to her', like it was a C-47! That did it! I skeedadled down the runway, weaving from side-to-side like a drunken sailor;

I was over-controlling and couldn't stop it. Becoming airborne before I was mentally ready only made matters worse. I was into a high-speed stall on the tree tops! Putting the nose back down gave me some control and a great deal of speed and by pulling on the stick a second time shot me up to 6,000 feet over the lake at Kunming before I knew it.

Then my primary training returned and my basic sense came back. I throttled back, lowered the gear and flaps, and got the 'seat of my pants' feeling. My landing was very uneventful. The next day I quit flying.

1st/Lt Ralph Parker
USAAF
0-796726

The Gurkhas Amazed Us

I was a Dakota pilot with 435 Squadron. I took my Initial Training in Canada, then went to England for a short time. I got my shots there, then along with several others went aboard one of those big 4-engined Sutherland flying boats—destination: India. When we arrived at Bahrain, in the Persian Gulf, we had to walk into a building, and good God was it hot! The hottest place I was ever at in my life. You could hold your hand out and just feel the heat coming off the sand. From there we went to Karachi and, finally, Rawalpindi where we took a 4-month training course on Dakotas.

One day we were out doing instrument-flying. We had a canvas over the pilot's position so he couldn't see anything. The navigator, a Polish chap from Winnipeg, was practicing blind-navigating. I was the second pilot and my job was to look ahead to make sure we didn't hit anything. I was ground-reading with a map just in case the navigator got all balled up and got lost.

Things were going OK until the navigator gave us the last leg to turn on to go back to base. I looked out the window, then I asked him, "Did you check your results on that?"

"Oh yah," he said, "We should be there in about 15 minutes."

"Well, I think you should check again, because in about 15 minutes we are going to run into a bit of a problem" I answered back.

So, he checked again and said, "Nah, that's Okay. We're right on course."

Then I said, "Well, I hate to disappoint you because there's something a little haywire here. In about 10 minutes we are going to run right smack into the Himalayan Mountains!"

The navigator was about 90 degrees off. We teased him after that. We told him that he (being Polish) just wanted to take us back to Russia—the hard way; over the mountains!

Once we got to Burma, our flying was quite close to the ground and our planes were so well camouflaged that when we flew over the forests we couldn't see the other Dakotas below us. If a Jap fighter was ever above us, he wouldn't be able to pick us out.

However, one time one of our pilots got over the dropping point when a Jap fighter spotted him and all the other Dakotas with him. As the fighter was coming down and getting ready to get the plane ahead of him, our pilot pulled up and flipped his wing tip up, thereby catching the Jap's wing tip. The fighter, being so light, flipped over and went straight into the ground. The Dakota was slightly damaged but was still flown home and the pilot received a DFC for his heroic action. I guess that's about all you could do with a Dakota because they weren't armed. The pilot might be given a revolver, but that was it.

Besides parachuting supplies to the British Army, we would parachute personnel, like the Gurkhas. They were short, wiry little fellows from the Himalayans and they had these special long knives. The Gurkhas, were excellent in close combat and really had a flair for jungle warfare. They would take those long, curved knives and chop heads off pretty quickly, let me tell you. Also, they were very loyal to the British and hated the Japanese.

We used to get Gurkhas to drop supplies and they absolutely amazed us. They'd sit there on the load, and they'd have their ball of wool and their knitting needles. On the way to the front they'd knit a sock and on the way back they'd knit the other sock. It always amazed us how fast they could knit a sock. They weren't issued any socks so they knitted their own.

You know, one thing really used to bug us. We used to fly all this beautiful Canadian beer into the British Army and meanwhile we Canadians were issued Indian and American beer. But every now and then we managed to keep a case or two of the good stuff for us. We used to haul about 6,000 pounds of it, all cased up in twenty-fours.

F/O Don MacLennan
RCAF
J42349

The Chin Hills in Burma, taken from an RAF Dakota, 1945.
— Irene Ord

THE GROUND CREWS

the unsung heroes of every squadron

You Can't Do That Yank!

The 31st Air Depot had arrived in Watton, England in October, 1943. The unit was housed in a tent city quickly erected on a sugar beet field about half a mile from the base where the unit was working. The men were restricted to camp, pending conversion of American money to British currency.

Our 19-man section was responsible for all weapons repair and supplies, turret and armament work for the ADG (Air Depot Group), weapons training for the troops and ground defense for the ADG.

After three days spent getting settled in the mud, cold and rain of England, an Air Force officer drove down to the tent city and converted all American money to British money. Each one of the men now had a pocket full of British pound notes, 10-shilling notes, and some of the strangest coins we had ever seen.

Naturally everyone wanted to see where we were stationed, to meet the British people and most of all to learn how to spend the new money we had. So off the troops went into the town of Watton and the nearest pub.

Since blackouts were enforced, the darkness was so thick one could almost cut it with a knife. We'll never forget the smell of burning coal as we walked the mile into town. Of course all the pub patrons were women and older men, as every man our age was already in the British military. Because of the absence of the younger men, the dartboard was idle.

Anyway, every Yank wanted to spend money to learn how to change, and almost refused to allow another buddy pay for a beer. One lad ordered a round of pints for all, but another Yank gave the innkeeper a pound note to pay for them. The young lad, determined to make the payment, to learn the currency system, grabbed the pound note from the innkeeper's hand. But in doing so, the bill was torn in two.

The innkeeper looked at the torn currency and said, "You can't do that Yank. That's the King's money."

Without thinking and possibly to show off in front of the local citizens, this lad replied, "To hell with the King's money, that's my money!"

Quiet fell upon the pub. No one spoke and the lad immediately knew that his exuberance and attitude were in poor taste. Next to the bar was an elderly gentleman wearing a tweed coat and smoking a pipe. He took a long draw from the pipe, exhaled and, looking the young Yank right in the eye, said, "And to HELL with Babe Ruth!"

T/Sgt Wile Noble
USAAF
ASN 34291252

Buzz Beurling was a Fun Guy

I went overseas at the age of 22 and worked with explosives in 401 Squadron, RCAF. I got a buck thirty a day plus ten cents an hour trade pay.

Captured German Me-109 at a German base near Fassburg, Germany, 1945.

Captured German Me-262, the first-ever jet combat aircraft, at a German base near Fassburg, Germany, 1945.

We used to work in shifts. Somebody always had to be on duty. You started work at 8 in the morning. The first thing you'd do was check the planes you were responsible for; our squadron flew Spitfires. You'd make sure the guns were working right, with the right amount of ammunition. Each pilot had his own idea of what he wanted to shoot from his guns. Most pilots would use a ratio of armour-piercing, tracer, two standard bullets, armour-piercing and a tracer. Some would prefer explosives.

Buzz Beurling, who flew with another squadron (412) but on the same drome as us, wanted nothing but armour-piercing, standard and explosives—no tracers. Yep, I worked on his plane. He was the No. 1 Canadian ace in the war and we got him after he already made his reputation with the RAF in Malta. He always said, "I don't need tracers. I know where I'm shooting. Just give me enough to do the job." Meanwhile, other pilots would want one tracer to five others, so they could tell where they were shooting. Every pilot was different.

After that bit of work was over you'd have some time to kill. You'd make sure the spare guns were working and set up the ammunition in case a pilot had to come back to the drome and rearm. We'd also hang bombs on the bottom of the fuselages and under the wings of the Spitfires. I was the first man to hang a 1,000-pound bomb on a Spitfire. This was done when we were getting close to D-Day and the pilots had to hit everything they could.

Buzz Beurling was a fun guy but a little weird. He was a great pilot and nobody could fly better. But they couldn't trust him as a squadron leader because he was just too undisciplined, and I'll give you an example of that.

We were in the southern part of England at a place called Redhill. Buzz shot down a plane that day and came back to base. He came across the drome, went up, did a 'victory roll' and landed. Of course, 'victory rolls' had been outlawed because too many very enthusiastic, second-class pilots couldn't do the roll and would kill themselves.

Redhill was just an English hayfield with a runway down the middle. When Buzz did his roll, the bottom of his prop was cutting the top of the hay which was about 5 feet high.

When his superiors saw this they said, "Look, you can't keep doing this. We know you can do it but a lot of other pilots will kill themselves trying. If you do it again we'll have to ground you". There was nothing Buzz hated more than being grounded.

A few days later Buzz shot down another Jerry. He came across the hayfield to do his victory roll and, sure enough, was cutting the top of the hay. This time he was upside down.

So, they pulled him up on the carpet and said, "We told you if you ever did that again we'll have to ground you."

Buzz snapped back, "I didn't do it the same way this time. I did it upside down!" That's Buzz Beurling.

Our squadron was in the D-Day Invasion, and I'll tell you a funny thing that happened to our sergeant major.

Being a sergeant major meant you got to leave the barge on a jeep while the rest of us had to leave on foot. He's on the barge next to us and there's water around and the beach right in front of us. The ramps dropped down and we all ran off and then off comes the sergeant major, as proud as could be, in his jeep. Well, what they didn't know was that they stopped the barge right in front of a shell hole but you couldn't see it under the water. So when he drove off the ramp, down he sank into the hole and completely disappeared—jeep and all! We thought he was a goner, but a few seconds later he swam out.

When we were on the continent, a couple incidents come to mind.

It was New Years Day, 1945, and the Germans were putting on a big push. They wanted to hit every drome they could get. We were at a place called Heesch. At another place, near Brussels, about forty Jerry fighters wiped out a drome. Most of our planes were on the ground when they got it. Three tried to get off and one did. This guy shot down two Germans before they finally got him.

When they came over our drome there were forty-two of them and they strafed us to bits. Luckily most of our planes had been out somewhere on a daylight-bombing run.

So when the Jerries came in again our Spits were returning and were right behind them.

Heesch, Holland. LAC Cecil Mann on right, loading 20mm shells into a Spitfire, with other ground crew member on the wing. Winter of 1944-45.

When the Jerries made their turns our guys drove right into them. We had a few planes on the ground which we had to take the bombs off, then send up. So we eventually had all our planes in the air.

Out of those forty-two planes, we shot down twenty-seven. Our planes actually shot down twenty-six. The other one was picked off by the ack-ack boys when one Jerry tried to follow two Spitfires as they were coming in to land. The ack-ack boys picked him off right between the two Spits!

Spitfire Comments

The Spitfires were never designed as a dive bomber; but we still strapped two 250-pound bombs under the wings and a 1,000 pounder in the belly, besides already having two cannons on the wings. Then we told the pilots to get going, and they did, too. They were never designed to do that, but it sure says a lot for the Spitfire.

LAC Cecil Mann
RCAF
R139202

A Flying Fortress on Auto-Pilot

I serviced Spitfires with 443 (Hornet) Squadron of the RCAF. We were the first all-Canadian fighter wing formed in England prior to the D-Day Invasion of France and our main concern was to maintain cover for the Canadian 1st Army.

Our fighter wing was completely mobile. We spent our time in England moving from one grass strip to another, for the experience we would need when the invasion took place. We lived in tents and slept on straw-filled mattresses with a ground sheet underneath. All the different trades, airframe-mechanics, armourers, electricians, and cooking staff, had their own trucks in order to be able to move with their equipment at a moment's notice.

Our squadron landed in Normandy on the third day of the invasion and we set up in a pasture field cleared of land mines. It was here our squadron came to be named the Hornet Squadron. When we arrived the days were hot and sunny and if we were eating outdoors, hornets would come and eat up all our jam rations.

One of the most humourous incidents that I recall, took place when we pitched our tents on the fringe of one of the first airstrips just inland from the invasion beach. Unknown to my buddy, Craig West of Ottawa, and myself, the Army moved in an anti-aircraft gun and camouflaged it so well that we didn't know it was there, that is until the air raids started. The gun was going full-tilt and the vibrations were pulling the tent pegs right out of the ground! So Craig grabbed a wooden mallet and, being safety-minded, put on his tin hat. There he was, stark naked and silhouetted by the illumination of the searchlights, pounding in tent pegs. I sure could've used my camera!

Another time an American Air Force B-17 (Flying Fortress) was on its return flight to England, after bombing a target in Germany. It was so badly shot up that the order to bail-out was given and it was set on auto-pilot, to head for and supposedly crash in the English Channel. Well, that bomber put on an aerial display for 30 minutes or more. It would climb almost straight up to a stall position, then it would go into a dive until we all thought it was going to crash. Then it would climb again. This was repeated many times, with only slight changes in its pattern. We finally sent two squadrons of Spitfires to shoot the Fortress down.

Getting the aircraft ready for the day's operations consisted of a visual check for oil or coolant leaks, and running the aircraft to check all gauges and insure everything was A-1.

Before any operations would start, two planes were sent up to check weather conditions. When in an active zone, as we were, the pilots had to be ready to scramble. Sometimes we had aircraft airborne in 27 seconds. Time was very important if enemy aircraft were sighted or an attempt to intercept was to be carried out.

Some days we would have our squadron escorting bombers on their runs to and from enemy territory. Occasionally, we even had a quiet day if the weather closed us in. On those days we would take a jeep and visit nearby villages, or stay on the airstrip to do laundry, write letters, or just relax. Our days were full of activity from dawn to dusk.

As we were in support of the Canadian 1st Army, we were just behind the front lines and a prime target for the German Luftwaffe.

We made a steady advance and were all anxious to reach Paris, which we did on September 7. From there we moved to Belgium and were set up in a civilian aerodrome just outside Brussels.

We had some great times in Brussels. But before we knew it our squadron advanced into Holland where we had to keep the only bridge capable of heavy traffic from being blown up—at Nijmegen. Our final move was to a German airfield, just outside of Hamburg. We took over the German barracks when the war came to a welcomed end.

Spitfire Comments

It had to be the ultimate in fighter aircraft. It had power, maneuverability and it arrived on the scene to give the RAF a much needed shot in the arm. Prior to the Spitfire, we were flying Fairey Battles and Hurricanes, in that order. While the latter two were good aircraft, they came up short when compared to the Messerschmitt and the Focke-Wulf.

The sound of the Spitfire, powered by a Rolls-Royce Merlin engine, in squadron formation or alone, was and still is something I will never forget.

LAC Vic Timmins
RCAF
R152180

What Took You So Long?

I'd like to recall a few incidents while I was with the 40th Bomb Group of the United States Army Air Forces.

I was stationed in Pratt, Kansas, where I was the crew chief of a B-17 Flying Fortress that was being used for training purposes. When the B-29 Superfortress arrived I became a crew chief on them.

My first maintenance crew consisted of one man who had finished Tech School on the B-29 but hadn't worked on it, an ex-fighter crew chief, one B-17 mechanic, and one ex-farmer. Our average time on the engines, at this time, was 25 hours. Usually, we worked 72 hours, and 5 hours of flying time. The first technical orders for maintenance that I saw were parts manual break-downs; no writing, just parts and part numbers. Progress from a maintenance view was very discouraging. My average day was about 20 hours on the 'flight line' with maybe 4 hours sleep on the hangar floor because I was too tired to walk to the barracks.

I departed Pratt in April, 1944, to ferry a B-29 to the Far East. I was the crew chief, flying with Captain Bill Hunter and crew. We flew to Presque Isle, Maine and landed with No. 3 engine out. After we repaired the engine and it stopped snowing, we departed for Gander, Newfoundland. We landed there with No. 2 out during a heavy snow storm. We found a clogged fuel filter and were quite fortunate to make Gander Bay, as the fuel filters on the other three engines were more than half plugged with foreign material. We spent about a week waiting for clear weather then departed for Marrakech, French Morocco.

Approximately one hour after take-off, No. 1 engine malfunctioned and we had to 'feather' it. All of Newfoundland and the east coast was socked in, so we had to continue on towards Africa on three engines. We had flown about 3 hours in this condition, gradually losing altitude, when No. 4 engine lost all power. I asked the flight-engineer, "What's happened?"

He said, "I don't know. I was shutting off the fuel to No. 1 engine and No. 4 stopped!"

I looked at the control panel and saw no fuel flow to No. 4 engine, so I pushed No. 4. fuel shut-off switch on and the engine resumed power. After getting No. 4 back up to power, I invited the engineer to vacate his seat. Then Captain Hunter and I started discussing our situation. We had about 1000 feet of altitude and were gradually losing that. I suggested we salvo the load of baggage and spare engine from the bomb bay. Then, if we couldn't maintain altitude we'd start throwing out the loose equipment. He agreed, but then said, "Let's try something else. My wife's picture is in my baggage."

I said, "OK, I am going to start up No. 1 engine and see if we can get enough power to stop our descent." With No. 1 engine started we managed to level out at about 500 feet and, as we burned fuel, we were able to climb to a more comfortable altitude.

During the time this was all going on the RH gunner called up and said, "Hey, No. 4 engine just blew up!"

I replied, "Damn, that's good!"

When we had time, we explained to the flight crew what had happened.

We landed in Marrakech and found the fuel filter on No. 1 engine was clogged. So we proceeded to pull fuel cell panels to inspect the inner fuel cells and found that someone had cleaned the inner cell with a lint rag.

We departed Marrakech for Cairo and landed in Cairo with No. 1 engine feathered—blown exhaust stacks! This was repaired and we spent about one week on the ground pulling a '50-hour inspection'. We departed Cairo for Karachi, India, but lost all but minimum power immediately after take-off. By flying through a mountain pass we were able to land at Oran, Algeria with one engine out again. On landing, we ruined one tire. Would you believe they didn't have a jack that would raise B-29? We had the base carpenter shop building us a ramp so we could *taxi* the plane up on it with one wheel and we changed the tire on the other wheel.

When we landed at Karachi we found we had blown exhaust stacks on No. 3 and No. 4 engines. These were repaired and we finished our ferry flight to Chakulia, India, landing with all four engines turning. When we got there, the ground crew wanted to know, "What took you so long?"

Superfortress Comments

The B-29 at the close of the war was a very good airplane, but when we first received it in 1943 and took it the China-Burma-India Theatre, was a *very* poor aircraft. I'm not sure, but I think everything on that airplane was changed or modified before the end of the war.

The Wright engine representative told me, when we were in India, that they had made 1800-plus modifications to the engine alone. The engines were the prime factors in our operational losses, because they were of *damn* poor design, and we didn't have the proper maintenance people to maintain them.

When we arrived in India, the allowable engine head temperature was 265 degrees. I never saw a temperature on the early B-29's that was under 300 degrees on take-off. As a result we were losing engines and aircraft on take-off. It wasn't uncommon to replace all top cylinders on the engines four or five times to try to reach the 400-hour limit on the engines. We also had a tremendous problem with exhaust stacks and collector rings. These would blow out and you either feathered the engine or risked the danger of a fire in the engine or nacelle.

M/Sgt Red Carmichael
USAAF
18004162

Halifax bomber getting an inspection

The crew of the Canadian-built Lancaster X, No. KB 777 with 428 Squadron RCAF. John Zinkhan is third from left.

'BOMB THE HUN!'

Bomber Command against Germany

German Ack-Ack

I was in No. 6 Canadian Heavy Bomber Command. While on operations, I was a navigator on both Halifaxes—five mine-laying operations—and Lancasters—twenty-seven raids. The latter consisted mainly of strategic targets in Germany, mostly in the Ruhr Valley, which contained most of Germany's heavy industry such as coal and iron as well as other manufacturing plants. It was probably the most heavily defended area in World War II from the stand-point of both heavy and light anti-aircraft artillery. The light ack-ack was quite deadly but most of the time we flew at heights which were out of its range.

The heavy ack-ack generally consisted of four 88mm cannons firing as a group. Each group was radar controlled. The radar obtained the aircraft's track, speed and height and from that 'predicted' where the aircraft would be when the bullets reached their height and position. The shells were set to explode at that point and didn't need to actually strike the aircraft to knock it down. In the heavily defended regions there would be many of these emplacements in an area. When we were on ops, the Germans had about 2,500 light ack-ack guns and 1,500 heavies in the Ruhr Valley alone.

The heavy ack-ack was unbelievably accurate, given good operators. I recall returning from a daylight raid, I believe on Stuttgart, on a course between the Terschelling Islands. They had gun emplacements at the ends of each of the Islands, so our course was exactly between the islands in order to stay as nearly out of range as possible. The ack-ack operators were both experienced and skillful, as well as very cagey. To indicate how important the accuracy of navigation was, we saw one of our aircraft flying slightly closer to one island than the other. The gun emplacement farthest away fired at the aircraft, which was slightly out of its range, but the bursts probably frightened the crew so that they veered away from them; right into the range of the nearer gun emplacement on the other island. The first burst brought down the aircraft. We never found out what happened to the crew.

One thing about flying heavy bombers, you never saw your friends actually die. They were just missing from the station the next day. Of course, this sort of thing resulted in a fatalistic attitude and the aircrews would go on some horrid benders whenever they were granted leave. This served to relieve the tension to some extent. Everybody was sure that the other fellow would 'go for the chop', never themselves. Everybody had some sort of a good luck charm, preferably obtained from some crew member who had completed a tour of operations.

Being a navigator, I must stress the importance of accurate navigation. When we were on 1,000-bomber raids, we were permitted a maximum of 3 miles off the pre-arranged track and a maximum of one minute off target. We were allotted a certain height and certain position in the mainstream. Considering that a thousand bombers took about 15 minutes over the target, from the first one to the last, it was amazing that more didn't run into each other when turning at right angles away from the target.

We were seldom more than a mile off track and only once more than a minute off target, and that time it was on purpose as we were at the tail end of the mainstream. If you got out of the mainstream the heavy ack-ack was able to predict you individually, with dire results. If you were

This is an Intelligence picture of the French coastline. The German defenses were softened up prior to D-Day. Note the bomb craters.
—RCAF

Air-to-air picture shots from John Zinkhan's aircraft on the way to a daylight raid on a flying bomb site. Actually, it was strictly forbidden to carry a camera in an operational aircraft.

Calais, France during a RCAF raid, 1944. —*RCAF*

This picture shows the tire size of the Lancaster in comparison to the 6-foot navigator, John Zinkhan, at left and the bomb-aimer, Bill Clark, at right.

in the mainstream, they were more or less flock shooting. The time we were a bit early, we noted that only one aircraft was behind us. Instead of losing more time purposely, by means of a dog-leg, we lost a bit less so as to stay in the mainstream. We noted a change in the forecast wind, which the rest of them didn't, except the one behind us.

They were really a good crew, on their second-last trip of their second tour. But perhaps they were a little too good, as the ack-ack were able to predict them and make a real mess of them. They managed to make it back to one of the emergency fields, but the pilot had his scalp laid back from his forehead to the back of his head, and the rest of the crew were badly battered up. The bomb-aimer, who was always the second pilot, flew the plane back and made a belly landing. The pilot received the immediate Distinguished Service Order and the rest of the crew received the immediate Distinguished Flying Cross (DSO and DFC). The powers that be awarded decorations in these situations in order to keep up the morale of the rest of the aircrews.

As for memories of actual operations, one of the most vivid is that of being attacked by a jet fighter, following a raid on Dortmund. We were lucky to escape that one. After dropping our bombs, the idea was to get the hell out in a hurry. The flight plan called for an approximate right angle turn, two minutes after dropping our bombs, then another approximate right angle turn, again to the left, two minutes later. Unfortunately, we turned the second time a minute late. This put us about 3 miles off the mainstream and permitted us to be predicted by the searchlights, which were controlled by radar. That is, the blue searchlight was controlled, and it switched on and caught us right in the middle. In no time at all, we were coned by about fifty searchlights. The normal procedure was for the 88mm guns to fire up the path of the blue searchlight, and that would be the end of the story. Much to our surprise this didn't happen. It turned out that about that period in the war the Germans had developed and put into production a jet fighter. The fighter defenses had vectored the jet onto us and told the ack-ack to remain quiet for fear of shooting down their own jet. It was also our good luck that they didn't have enough fuel at that time to properly train their jet fighter pilots.

We put the nose of the aircraft down, with all four Rolls-Royce Merlin engines at 2,000 horsepower each on full-boost and maximum RPM, at the same time using the prescribed evasive tactics for ack-ack predicted fire. In a few minutes our rear-gunner spotted the jet and fired a few hundred rounds which didn't apparently bother the fighter. However, he must have been going too fast to properly bring his guns to bear on us, so he had to turn and make a full 360-degree circuit to get at us again. As luck would have it he must have misjudged his speed, which was phenomenal compared to previous fighters, so he never did get another pass at us. Meanwhile, we had our Lanc travelling at about 425 miles-per-hour ground speed so it didn't take too long to get out of the searchlights. It only took a few minutes, but it seemed like ten days. The Lanc was travelling so fast that the combined efforts of the bomb-aimer and pilot couldn't pull it out of the dive; the controls were frozen due to the excessive speed. Somebody finally decided to trim it out by using the trim tabs on the ailerons. So with bull strength and the trim tabs, we finally got straight and level. Nobody needs to tell me that luck isn't important in life!

We had a number of interesting situations while on ops. One time we were attacked by a day fighter while on a night operation. We had a compass failure, which was unusual as we were equipped with distant-reading compasses as well as the P4 magnetic compass. The DR compass was situated near the back of the aircraft. It was about as big as an 8-gallon milk can. Basically, it was a gyroscopic compass and the precessing was controlled by electric 'kicks', in turn directed by a magnetic compass. Normally it was very accurate. Instead of giving the compass reading, which was subject to magnetic variation as well as deviation due to electrical components and aircraft design, both of which were in a continuous state of change as the aircraft flew over different geographical areas and in different directions, it read the actual true readings, incorporating the various changes as it went along. Also, the DR compass had repeaters in the navigators' and pilots' compartments, although the main machine was near the back of the aircraft.

Before we realized that the DR compass was in fact precessing without being corrected, we had already flown over the North Sea and all the navigational calculations were naturally haywire. The calculated winds were wrong, the calculated TMG (track made good) was wrong and by that time we were out of effective Gee-range with no way of getting a good positional fix.

To digress for a moment, we were equipped with two types of radar: the Gee and the H2S. Both were supposed to be highly secret but naturally the Germans knew all about them. In fact, they were at times effectively able to jam the Gee signals.

The Gee system consisted of three ground-based broadcasting stations: one master and two slaves. The master would broadcast a signal, which in turn was rebroadcast to each of the slaves. The slaves were located a certain distance away and in a certain position, so that the end result was that a small box about the size of a 5-pound box of chocolates was able to receive blips. These in turn were transferred to position lines on a special map. Crossing the position lines on the map gave you an almost perfect fix or position.

The H2S, on the other hand, was broadcast from the aircraft itself. The whole set of equipment weighed something like 2,800 pounds. It would broadcast signals to the ground, which in turn were bounced back and received by the aircraft. Things such as buildings gave a stronger reflection than trees or water. Cities were normally easy to pick up, as well as rivers, coastlines and lakes.

With compass failure, we decided to fly on the P4, but by that time we were almost completely lost. We finally managed to pick up a fix on a small lake in Norway. This was on a trip to Stettin, one of the longest. We were able to alter course directly to the target, but by that time were something like 30 miles off track, and that far out of the mainstream.

The ack-ack in that area was almost non-existent but they managed to vector a fighter onto us. Fortunately he was still carrying day-tracers. He missed on his first burst and his own bright day-tracers must have blinded him so that he never got another run at us. Incidently, through a bit of navigational skullduggery, we managed to hit the target on time and were able to get into the mainstream on the way back.

Lancaster Comments

The Lancaster X, on which I did most of my operational flights, was a wonderful machine. It was quite maneuverable. In fact, the Germans called it the 'four-engined fighter'. As aircrew

The Avro Lancaster in flight

officers, we found this out through our access to intelligence data; but that's another story. As a result of the Lanc's 8,000 horsepower, we were able to climb with a full bomb load at the rate of 1,000 feet-per-minute. This was advantageous to us as we were able to fly close to the water until we hit the enemy coast, then climb rapidly to bombing height. By avoiding radar, the Germans were unable to predict our expected target early enough and thereby couldn't vector their fighters onto us.

A good part of the engines' efficiency was related to the paddle-blade propellers which were developed to replace the toothpick props. Also, they were much more efficient, especially at higher altitudes, part of this due to the system of supercharging the engines. Gas mileage was about one mile-per-gallon. The engines were very reliable; in fact, the only work done to ours were changes to the oil, the spark plugs and the magnetos.

F/L John Zinkhan
RCAF
J25044

The 'Push On Crew'

What a crew we were! A bunch of clods and clots! I, for one, wasn't that good a pilot. Some of my landings were just terrible. Bump, bump, bump, before I'd finally settle down for good. But when I had to make a good landing after a rough night where the flak was unusually heavy and the Halifax came back all full of holes, then my landings were perfect. Nice and smooth.

The navigator was a real gem. An alcoholic. Not just a hard drinker, but an alcoholic. When we'd leave England on the way to Germany, he was so loaded that he was no use to us. But once we got near the target he turned into a different person. Letter perfect! He was, without a doubt, a great navigator who really knew his job. But once we turned around for our return trip he became his old self; he'd fall asleep over the Channel and we'd have to land on our own. Myself and the other crew members overlooked some of his problems because he always got us over the target and he was great over enemy territory.

Our mid-upper gunner, a Cockney fellow who we called 'Duff-Gen Harry', would always give us the wrong direction of any approaching fighter. If the fighter was off the port side, he'd say it was off the starboard. If the enemy flew an Me-109, he'd say it was a Focke-Wulf. He had such a terrible accent we could barely understand him.

What a crew! But you know, when our squadrons photo-flash snapshots—76 Squadron RAF—were pinned on the bulletin board the day after a raid (these were the pictures that each bomber had taken when the bombs hit the ground) our crew was either in the top three or we weren't there at all. We were that close to the target! Only bad weather or mechanical problems would keep us from finishing near the top. I'm not bragging either, it's a fact. That was quite an achievement for a dumb crew like us.

I remember one flight in particular. We were coming out of England and were somewhere over the North Sea. Around that time the German night fighters would work in pairs. One would drop a bright flare, either red or yellow, which would light up a very wide area. Then the other fighters would pick out the bombers and go after them. I saw five of our own bombers get shot down this way, right in front of me. I lost consciousness and I don't know how long I was in that condition. The next thing I knew I could hear the tail-gunner yell, "There's a Focke-Wulf on our tail . . . . corkscrew to port, GO!" And down I took the plane into a corkscrew.

The fighter was smart. He stayed outside the range of our .303's which was about 600 yards, and waited till we got to the top of our corkscrew. When this happens the plane shudders with any full bomb-load, and that's when the fighter hits us with his cannon fire at 1,000 yards. He shot off the starboard wing-tip and set a starboard engine in flames!

To get rid of the fighter and the flames, I took the bomber into a wild dive; but as I did the controls froze on me! It took three of us, the bomb-aimer, the flight-engineer, and myself, to pull back on the controls to bring it out. The speedometer read 425 miles-per-hour! As we were going down the tail-gunner shot the pursuing Focke-Wulf right out of the sky.

We levelled out at 8,000 feet and had a conference. I was worried about flying to the target at such a low altitude, where I'd be easy prey for flak, fighters and the bombs from our own planes which would be another mile or two above us. So I said over the intercom, "Well, what do you think men? Should we go on?"

"Push on skipper," they said, one at a time. That was us, by the way, the 'push on crew'. And I was known as the 'Gremlin' because I used to pull the flaps up on my helmet so that they looked like ears sticking out.

So, we got to our target and we sure must've been late because we were the only bomber in the sky. But that didn't bother us. We barrelled right through the centre and dropped our bombs. When we pulled out a Ju-88 came at us, port to starboard. Our bomb-aimer shot at him and missed, but the tail-gunner fired a few rounds and he might've got him, too, because he later received a 'probable'. One 'certain' and one 'probable' was good shooting for one night.

After the raid we're lumbering along in our disabled craft, losing height. I could see an ack-ack barrage in the distance, and there was no way around it. So I just put the nose down, to gain speed, and went right through the shell fire. We could hear the shells exploding— BOOM . . . . BOOM! One got too close because our hydraulics, we soon found out, were gone. That meant we'd have trouble landing because the wheels and flaps wouldn't work.

Soon we could see the coast and more anti-aircraft fire. I put the nose down a second time and flew right through the fire again. No direct hits.

Now we were over the water and those white caps looked close and we couldn't gain any height! I called out, "Dinghy, dinghy. Prepare for ditching!" We might have to go down in the drink. We had only three minutes to get out of the plane and into the dinghy after it was automatically inflated once the plane hit the water.

We were all thinking about our individual jobs once the plane would touch the water surface. Then suddenly the bomb-aimer screams, "Light directly ahead!" We were approaching England!

Our IFF was shot away and I was worried about getting shot down over England before we could be properly indentified.

There we were, no flaps or wheels working and no IFF. The land was coming up fast, we were going 200 miles-per-hour, and just before hitting the ground I shut the petrol off so the plane wouldn't catch fire. We plowed into the ground and slid for awhile, hit a hedge and stopped. The props were smashed, the rear-gunner unconscious and the Halifax was an utter mess! A total write off. A million dollar aircraft destroyed.

We slept that morning in full gear at a nearby house, right on the living room floor, and when we got up we made our way back to base.

Halifax Comments

We knew the Lancaster flew higher, faster, carried a bigger bomb-load and had more armament. It was a better bomber than the Halifax, but we never admitted it to those Lancaster crews. The Halifax was a good plane, you know. It got me through thirty-six missions.

F/L Clifford Waite
RCAF
R141733

Flying into Our Own Bomber Stream

Being a tail-gunner was terribly monotonous. My first trip was to Chemnitz, a 10-hour trip. Ten hours in the air with nothing to do. So I used to count rivets, and there's a few thousand in a Halifax bomber! I even had the counts sectionalized. Other things used to bug me, though, like the heated flying suits. They contained gloves, shoes and a body warmer. But sometimes the suits would short out on you which left you with a hot spot. You had to turn off the brute until you got cold, then turn it back on again.

That raid on Chemnitz was quite unique, besides being my first, because I got a good view of it. That time our navigator got all crossed up and we ended up flying directly into our own

The crew of OW-E. from l to r: Tom Lightly, flight-engineer; Joe Wilks, wireless-operator; Ted Boek, bomb-aimer; Dick Reith, pilot; Jack Sklar, mid-upper gunner; Jim Baker, navigator; Linc Johnson, tail-gunner.

bomber stream. I saw Focke-Wulf 190's and Me-109's and we were going the wrong way. Then we had to come back on our own because we were out of the stream. We went down to the deck and gave full-throttle all the way back to our base at Linton-on-Ouse in England. The engines were pretty well shot after that run. On the raid we were coned in searchlights over the Ruhr Valley, so the pilot took the plane into a severe dive and the Germans, for some reason, shut the lights off. That was our first trip.

I flew with 426 Squadron, commonly known as the Thunderbird Squadron. I went on twenty-eight trips but never completed the required thirty because the war ended. About a dozen of these raids were in daylight. We would fly at around 21,000 feet and had lots of fighter-cover above us; Mustangs and Mosquitos to help out the bomber stream. You never really knew the fighters were there because they'd be up at around 30,000 feet. But if any German fighters came at you, then our boys would come down.

I remember a trip when one of those German rocket-powered planes (the Me-163 Komet) came through our formation and shot the tail off a Lancaster. But when our fighters dived down to get him, the German left them standing still since the Komet could travel close to 600 miles-per-hour.

We had our own plane most of the time. OW-E were the letters, but we called it OW-Easy. I had my own guns. I'd check them before take-off by rotating the turret around and around and looking at the ammo tracks to make sure they wouldn't jam. After that I'd jump out and wait till we got the word to go.

A notable mission took us to Helgoland, an island south of Denmark in the North Sea, where a number of German sub pens were located. I saw the before-and-after pictures of that raid. There was a little town on it and an airfield. But when we got finished with it, it looked like a plowed field! As we approached the island, anti-aircraft fire came up but after a couple of minutes they quit. They must've ran for their air-raid shelters.

Halifax Comments

It was a good aircraft. It didn't carry the weight the Lancaster did, but it hung together. It was tough, and could take a lot of abuse. I saw one guy get a 500-pound bomb stuck in his wing from a plane above, it didn't go off luckily, and he brought it back to base. In fact, our craft once got hit by incendiaries and we got home, too.

Another pilot was doing an evasive-action, a corkscrew as we called it, and just when he started to climb in the corkscrew a flak shell exploded under the craft and it flipped right over on its back. The Halifax was not built to stand upside-down flying, but he came back, too. The wings were all wrinkled up from the stress, but it still touched down.

F/Sgt Linc Johnson
RCAF
R209960

Sometimes The Guns Would Jam

I flew thirty-seven ops as a tail-gunner without having to fire a single bullet in combat. We were on Halifaxes with 432 Squadron, RCAF.

On ops, we'd spend six weeks on bombing-raids, then take one week off to cool down a bit and take a well-deserved rest.

One day our squadron was doing circuits-and-bumps. Just before one of our take-offs, one tire ran off the tarmac, which was about 4 inches above the ground. The tires, back then, weren't all that good and the instant that happened the tire pinched against the tarmac causing a blow-out. The plane immediately started to pull to one side. We took it up but when the pilot tried to pull the undercarriage up, the tire flapped around and caused such a terrible vibration that I could feel the jarring all the way to the tail-section. We managed to land the next time around at about 90 miles-an-hour and the plane whipped to one side, but the pilot managed to hang on and we came to a stop.

Did you know that we never used the same Halifax on all those ops? We had to take a different plane every time, which can cause a lot of problems for every crew member. In my case, if I had the same plane each time, then I'd be responsible for my own guns and I'd make sure they were in proper working order. I'd clean them and I'd make darn sure they'd fire properly. One time I went on a mission with none of the four rear-turret guns in serviceable order. Sometimes the guns would jam and other times they didn't have enough ammo.

Halifax Comments

On my last mission, a 4,000-pound 'Cookie' from one of the bombers above went right through our fuselage. A gaping hole, top to bottom, but the pilot still kept us in the air for another seven or eight minutes. We were losing about 1,000 feet-per-minute. If that had happened to another bomber, like the Lancaster, it might've gone down right away. The Lancaster could carry those 22,000-pound Grand Slams, but they had to suffer some in bottom-end strength in order to carry the big bomb-loads. The Halifax seemed tougher.

F/O Mike Harrington
RCAF
J92231

The Panicky Tail-Gunner

It took teamwork to finish a tour of ops. Every crew member had to concentrate on his job; pilot, navigator, bomb-aimer, gunners. And with a little bit of luck, a tour could be completed.

I navigated on thirty missions, a complete tour, with 115 Squadron of the RAF out of Witchford, England, near Cambridge. Everyone on our crew finished the tour with me except the tail-gunner, and that's a story in itself.

We were flying at 22,000 feet when, without warning, we were coned in searchlights. To get rid of them we had to take a very severe dive. But when we did that the intercom battery shook loose and flew off its usual place and that's where the confusion started. All communication with one another was now gone. The crew members near the front of the plane knew what was happening but I don't think the tail-gunner did. Being so far away from the rest of us and unable to communicate, he must've thought we took a shell and started going down.

Meanwhile, the pilot finally got rid of the cones and trimmed the Lancaster out at 800 feet. Then the wireless-operator found the battery and put it back in place. Everything seemed under control, or so we thought.

Now to see if the intercom was working, the pilot asked each member if everything was back to normal.

When he got to the tail-gunner, there was no answer.

The wireless-operator went to the back of the plane, then came back a short time later and said, "Hey skip, the back door's open! He's gone!" I wonder what the tail-gunner must've thought as he parachuted down and we flew right past him.

P/O Alan Hall at the nav. desk of his Lancaster, 1944.

A ground crew member and tail-gunner Bob Barr at the tail section of their Lancaster, Witchford, England, 1944.

When I joined the RAF I tried to get in as a pilot, but they wouldn't accept me. They said my vision was not good enough. 'Perception of Depth' they called it. I went to a navigation class at Crumlin Airport (now London Airport). There were fifty-two of us in all and only four finished a complete tour. Mind you, some went into Ferry Command where they didn't have to face combat, but not too many from our group. From Crumlin I went to England.

Once, while at OTU in England, we were flying Wellingtons and our skipper forgot to lower the undercarriage. When we hit the runway the Wellington caught fire right away. The crew members in the front of the plane, like myself, got out the hatch by climbing on the pilot's shoulders and through the opening just above us. But our second navigator, who was along for training purposes, and the rear-gunner were both burnt to death!

Once I made ops a couple of things immediately come to mind. In the morning we'd all look on the board to see if we were flying that day. If we were then we'd have to start preparing ourselves. Later on we'd get briefing and the navigators would go in first, about a half-hour before everyone else because we had to chart our course. Then the other crew members would come in.

After dispersal it was hard because you had to wait before boarding the bombers. And that was bad, because the waiting could kill you! Your nerves could get to you, but once I got on the plane I was too busy to get nervous.

The second thing I remember were the night fighters. They'd come at you from behind, and if the tail-gunner spotted one he'd yell, "Starboard go!" And down we'd go into a corkscrew to evade the fighter. Most of the time the fighter was too fast and he'd sail right past; that's if your tail-gunner saw him first. If he didn't, then you'd get shot up! That was the secret to it; spot him first. You can see why everyone had to do his job to last a tour.

Lancaster Comments

The best plane in the whole darn war. Very maneuverable for a big four-engined bomber. One time we were over England when we met a B-17 Flying Fortress, so we decided to have a friendly little dogfight. Yes, a dogfight with bombers! We could keep on his tail, but he couldn't keep on ours.

P/O Alan Hall
RCAF
J90801

Landing on Three Engines

Once I made operations, fifteen in all, I took a certain pride in my landings. I wanted them as smooth as possible. The crew of my Lancaster and I went through a little ritual on every landing. The wireless-operator went to the rear of the fuselage, and sat on the Elsan toilet. If he got splashed when I touched down, then I had to buy beer for the whole crew.

On a particular night-raid over Germany a shell knocked out our inner-starboard engine and it immediately spun to the ground. But, when we got back over British territory my crew still demanded the usual ritual, with no excuses. One less motor didn't seem to matter, at least not to them. But this time the landing was far from perfect, and the wireless-operator took a splashing as he sat at his usual touch-down position.

When we landed and opened the hatch, I was met by a not-too-happy ground-crew chief who commented, "Would you please tell me how I'm going to replace a whole engine? I'm having enough trouble just getting lightbulbs for the barracks, unless I take some of the old bulbs back." I told him I couldn't do anything about it because I had left the engine somewhere outside Berlin. That still didn't seem to satisfy him but 48 hours later the motor was replaced!

Lancaster Comments

What a beautiful machine to fly. It was comfortable and very maneuverable, not slow or sluggish. It could climb quite easily on three engines and in a pinch could do the same on two engines, although those Merlins would sure be revving.

The first time I sat in the pilot's seat and flew that baby, it seemed that I and the Lancaster were one. The Lanc' was the sweetest thing that ever lived.

RAF

I Don't Remember a Thing

We were just kids back then. I was only 17 when I joined the RCAF; that was back in December of '42. The following January I turned 18 and a month later they called me up. On January 14, 1944, while in PEI, I received my wings in October of the same year I went on ops. I was a mid-upper gunner on Lancasters with 626 Squadron, out of Wickenby.

Back in '42 when I went to the recruiting office, I told them I wanted to be a gunner. One reason was that my dad was a machine-gunner in the First World War. My training involved taking apart the guns and putting them back together, and Morse Code study to help the pilot locate or identify land marks.

My first operation, on the 7th of October, 1944, was a daylight raid on Emmerich. This was just before the Allies crossed the Rhine. I can remember seeing Spitfires, Hurricanes and American P-38's flying with us as fighter support.

When we dropped our bombs, the bomb-aimer shouted over the intercom, "Bombs gone. Now let's get out of here!" But as we turned to get back to England we caught a load of 10-pound incendiaries from the plane above. One bomb went through the tail fin, one went through the back part of the fuselage and hung inside the body, while a few others smashed into both wings where the gas tanks were, causing both engines to pour out fierce, black smoke. To this day I still don't know why those incendiaries didn't blow the whole plane apart.

We still managed to fly after that, although with some difficulty and with the constant fear of exploding in mid-air. As we made our way back to base, the pilot tried to touch-down at the emergency landing strip which was just off the coast, but due to cloud cover we overshot and continued on to our home base at Wickenby. The pilot, F/O Rod Clement from Manitoba, received the DFC for bringing the kite home.

My second op, October 19, 1944, was the big raid on Stuttgart with 1,000 bombers. According to my log, take-off time was 12:17 hours and the flying time was 7 hours 14 minutes. The first wave hit at 7 PM, and we were supposed to come in with the second wave at 8 PM. By the time we got there the city was in flames! Fires all over the place!

On our way back, I shouted, "Where are we?"

"Over France. Why?", the navigator replied.

"I see some concentrated flak off our tail!"

After that I don't remember a thing. Not a thing! I heard later that the plane crashed on touch-down and cut the middle section right in half, just in front of the mid-upper turret, and one wing broke off, too. I suffered a fractured skull and back injuries. That was it for my ops; just two. I never got up in the air again, at least not in combat.

Lancaster Comments

You had to be small, and I was at 120 pounds, to fit in the turret of a Lancaster. There was more room in the mid-upper turret than the tail-turret, but even with all your gear on it was still pretty tight.

The Lancaster was a fine aircraft. During training our pilot had to fly it on only one engine, with all us crew aboard, and it did OK.

F/Sgt Robert Richmond
RCAF
R208457

The crew with Sgt Bob Hide when they were flying Stirlings with 199 RAF Squadron. Back row r to l: P/O Tom Kyle pilot; Bill Bristow, engineer; F/O Bill Humphreys, navigator; F/Sgt Cyril Hughes, tail-gunner**. Front row: Sgt Bob Hide, wireless-operator; Frank Shields, mid-upper gunner*; F/Sgt Jack MacDonnell, bomb-aimer.*

*these two men did not go on the flight described.
**the only other crew member to come out alive besides Bob Hide.*

'We're going Down!'
—bomber crews shot down over Germany

The Lancaster Became an Inferno

It all started on a dispersal on my squadron's airfield. The crew of *O for Orange*, which included myself, was standing by the aircraft waiting for the appointed hour when we would take off for our tenth sortie over enemy territory.

The target chosen for that night was the very heart of the Reich; Berlin. As this was our first sortie over the 'Big City', there was a lot of speculation as to the opposition we would encounter because the city's defenses were reputed to be very heavy. However, we were not deterred by the reputation of the city and we made bets, with the odd coppers remaining in our pockets, as to the number of fighters likely to be seen that night.

The time arrived for donning our flying kit and we climbed into our Lancaster. When everyone had checked his equipment, the four great Merlin engines were started. Then one by one all the aircraft in the other dispersal started and rolled forward to the take-off point.

One by one the aircraft rolled down the mile and a half of runway, with engine throttles wide open. About three-quarters of the way down the runway, they took to the air and gradually disappeared into the dusk. We were the second aircraft to take off and, with a final wave to the crowd, we started down the runway and became airborne.

The crew of *O for Orange* and their duties were as follows. The skipper, Thomas Kyle, was a good-looking and carefree 23 year old Australian. His duties consisted of flying the aircraft and the responsibility to the crew and aircraft during the sortie.

Our navigator, a 21 year old Welshman named Bill Humphreys, was to know the position of the aircraft at all times and had to get us to the target on time.

Jack McDonnell, aged 25 and also an Australian, did the bomb-aiming. His job consisted of helping the navigator with map reading and to release the bombs over the aiming-point.

The next member was the engineer. Our own engineer, Jack Grout, fortunately for himself, was unable to accompany us on this trip. The man with us at the time was on his first sortie and I didn't get his name. His job was to look after the engines and see that the petrol was used to the best advantage.

Frank Shields, the regular mid-upper gunner, got a touch of the flu and his place was taken by another chap.

The rear-gunner was a New Zealander named Bill Hughes. His job, combined with the mid-upper gunner, was to defend the aircraft against all fighter attacks and to warn the crew of any impending danger.

The only remaining member was myself, as wireless-operator. My job was to keep in touch with our base in England.

After taking off, we circled to gain height and after a little while we set course for the enemy coast. The daylight had gone and one could see nothing but dim outlines of other aircraft at different heights, all headed in the same direction—their red and green navigation lights glowing like rubies and emeralds embedded in black velvet.

The moon was not due to rise until an hour after we set course and it was almost full when it finally did rise. The sky was cloudless. By this time we had crossed the English coast and were well out over the North Sea.

At about 8:15 PM the first plane crossed the coast, which was confirmed by the sighting of flak bursts and searchlights. We crossed the coast at approximately 8:20; but owing to the wind being faster than first thought, all the aircraft were 'off track' and the crossing was made at the wrong place. This proved our undoing.

Bill, the navigator, asked the skipper to fly a straight-and-level course to enable him to obtain a position. Up to this point we had been dodging and weaving the flak and searchlights as we always did.

When we started the level flight, we were just south-west of Kiel. Suddenly there was a heavy, dull thud followed by a blinding flash which lit the interior of the aircraft. The aircraft's nose immediately turned earthward and we headed down in a steep dive.

The interior of the Lancaster became an inferno, and I received severe burns to my hands and slight burns to my face. During this time I was off the intercom, so I failed to hear what was going on in the other parts of the aircraft. By now, it was impossible to put the flames out because they had really taken hold.

I could barely see the navigator through the smoke. He was moving to the front hatch with his chute clipped on, so I presumed that the order to 'bail out' was given. I reached for my chute which was just behind me. This caused my right hand to become burned worse than it already had been.

The fixing of my chute was somewhat difficult because my hands were skinless; dead skin hung from my palms and wrists. However, with my chute on, I worked my way forward to the pilot. Tommy had one leg out of the seat but by still hanging onto the stick, he kept the aircraft level.

Mac, Bill and the engineer were down in the hatchway trying to open the hatch when, without warning, the aircraft exploded and started to disintegrate. I was thrown forward into the bombing compartment, half unconscious. From then on things were hazy. I do remember finding the nose completely missing and Bill standing with his back against the wall of the aircraft. I shouted to him to jump. Then I stepped through the hole where the nose had been, but my foot caught in some twisted framework and I found myself hanging onto the remains of the aircraft.

I wrenched my foot free and simultaneously pulled the ripcord of my chute. I judged our height at about 1,500 feet because the flames illuminated the fields below the size of a football pitch.

Just after leaving the aircraft I went unconscious and didn't 'come to' until prior to hitting the ground. I was travelling in a backward direction, my heels hitting first, then down on my head, cutting it badly. All the wind had been knocked out of my body and I waited a minute or so before I could do anything.

My first action on regaining my breath was to rid myself of my chute and harness. I rose from the ground with some difficulty and found that the Lancaster had landed only 10 yards away. I staggered past the wreckage which was still burning in some places and made my way to a road. I saw nothing of the crew and presumed them all dead.

I followed the road which ran along the top of a hill, and seeing a river and feeling very thirsty I broke through a hedge to get a drink. On reaching the bank I laid down and dipped my face in, drinking at the same time.

Up to now my hands had not troubled me much, except for some throbbing. I thought the water would ease the pain, so I put them in the stream. This proved to be very foolish. When they entered the water the pain became unbearable.

I left the river and started to walk again. I was still very dazed by the sudden event of things and shortly afterwards I found myself back at the place I started from so I decided to try the opposite direction. After walking 50 yards or so, the outline of a building came in sight.

A figure loomed in front of me, so I shouted to him that I was with the RAF and an Englander. He led me to a barn, opened the door and called to a woman inside who flicked on the electric light. Inside, besides herself, were two children and two horses. The woman and children were somewhat frightened which didn't surprise me, because the Lancaster had crashed only 50 or 60 yards away.

Stirling Comments

Although the Stirling isn't mentioned in this log, I did fly ops with it—199 Squadron—before switching to the Lancaster on 7th Pathfinder Squadron. I must say that the Stirling was my first love for a few reasons, besides being my first operational plane.

The crew comfort was excellent. The cockpit contained pilot and co-pilot seats which the Lancaster did not—only a pilot seat. In fact, you could quite easily fit three abreast in the Stirling. It also had ⅜ inch armour plating in the exposed positions, such as the cockpit and the gun positions. And during an evasive-action corkscrew (a sudden drop to the left or right and moving in a circle to get away from enemy fighters) the aircraft was very acrobatic. It could dive straight down very suddenly and almost leave your stomach in your throat.

Lancaster Comments

Besides being a better fighter, it would fly another 5,000 feet higher than the Stirling. I remember on some missions when we could look down and see the Stirling flying far below us, which made our crew feel much safer at our 20,000 feet.

The Lancaster, believe it or not, could fly on one engine. It couldn't climb on one, but it could maintain altitude if the Lanc was in trouble.

It certainly didn't have crew comforts. The cockpit, for instance, seated only the pilot. No co-pilot. And the other positions seemed cramped. It was not a roomy aircraft.

The Lancaster could evade enemy fighters, but you couldn't try the same corkscrewing methods that the Stirling could do. I can still remember when I switched to the Lancaster, after a handful of ops on the Stirling. You didn't just jump from one type of plane to another, you had to go through some training. The instructors told us that the Lancaster was not the same aircraft as the Stirling. They told us not to try the same type of corkscrewing, evasive-action techniques because if you did you would twist the twin tail-rudders right off. The Lanc had to evade a little more smoothly. Any pilot who wasn't listening to this advice soon found out the hard way; in the air.

The bomb load on both aircraft was about equal, in the 12,000 pound range.

WO₁ Bob Hide
RAF
1392048

Four Feet Missing Off The Wing

After navigator training at Malton and instructing at Portage la Prairie, I went directly to further training in England in April of 1944.

Right away they asked me, "What do you want to do?"

I said, "I want to be a Pathfinder", and I really wanted to be one because Pathfinders were an elite group.

I spent three weeks at Pathfinder Force Navigational Training Unit and I enjoyed the training because of excellent instructors who made it all so easy. It was here that I was paired with an English chap named Whitaker, and we were trained as a navigational team.

On completion of training, we were posted to 582 RAF Pathfinder Squadron at Little Staughton and joined the crew of Flight Lieutenant Thomas. Because I went to Pathfinder Training and then directly onto a squadron as a replacement, I got on ops very quickly and I missed taking OTU and other training which would have taken the better part of a year.

Incidentally, our crew consisted of six English Air Force types and myself, the only Canadian. From then on I told them that the six of them equalled one Canadian anyway.

My best story, or the one I remember the best, was the day I was shot down. I remember quite a few other happenings, but that day really stands out.

The time was December 23, 1944, and I was about to go on my twenty-first operation. It was going to be a day raid and a special mission; not a regular Pathfinder operation. We were briefed four mornings in a row for this raid because the weather the previous three days was terrible. By now everybody must've known we were to hit the Cologne marshalling yards and we were going to do it on OBOE.

On OBOE there was a lead aircraft, in this case a Lancaster, and it was controlled by two ground-radar stations in England that zeroed it onto the target, with the rest of us Lancasters playing follow-the-leader. On this mission there were going to be three groups of eight flying double-line astern and four to a side. We had to fly into the target straight-and-level for six minutes, with the bomb doors wide open.

The morning of the raid, when I picked up my parachute, I noticed there was a piece sticking out from the chute and I didn't like that one bit, so I took it back. The girl there was rather annoyed, but too bad for her. I didn't want that piece catching on something and shredding it to bits, if I ever had to use the chute.

We had briefing that morning and took off in heavy overcast skies. Once we left the deck (runway), we formed up for our mission to Cologne.

When we got over France everything was fine except for one detail; we were four minutes ahead of time. Now remember I said there were three groups of eight, twenty-four of us, and we were supposed to be the second group over the target. But as it turned out we weren't; we were going to be the first! Some P-51 Mustangs were supposed to provide cover but we were even 2 minutes ahead of them! So there we were, with no fighter cover and ahead of time; flying double-line astern and straight-and-level; easy pickings on enemy radar.

Then to make matters worse, when we were 5 minutes from the target, beautiful sunshine broke through. As you can see, nothing was working for us that day. Right away we were attacked by German fighters; thirty-nine to be exact. The two Lancasters behind us got hit, then

P-51 Mustang in combat

the one opposite us, then us. I could distinctly remember a cannon shell ripping through the plane and I could smell the cordite. Also, there was a fire in the bomb-bay, but we pressed on and dropped our bombs on the target.

By this time our port-outer and starboard-inner engines were shot up and we were losing altitude. The tail-gunner managed to shoot down an enemy fighter and a P-51 came to our rescue and shot down another. Meanwhile the mid-upper gunner, a Canadian who filled in for this trip, was hit and badly wounded.

The skipper regained control of the Lancaster and held her somewhat steady at around 4,000 or 5,000 feet. Things were getting hectic by now! I reached to get my chute when I noticed it was laying about 6 inches away from a large flak hole. Darn, was I lucky it didn't fall through! Whitaker, the second navigator, couldn't find his chute so he and I looked for it until we found it. The mid-upper gunner, who I said was wounded, somehow pulled his chute in the plane and it was all over the place. I said that we should bundle the chute up and throw him out just like that, but he didn't like my suggestion. Then I said the two of us could jump out on my chute, but he didn't like that either. Then he said he'd rather stay in the plane with the pilot and take his chances.

I was hanging on to a hand rail when suddenly I heard a crash. I looked up and there, only 6 feet away, was a 4-foot hole. Then I looked out the door and saw about 4 feet missing off one of the wings. On the inside the hydraulics were all shot away. What a mess!

I helped the mid-upper to the cockpit and then I went to the back of the plane. The rear-gunner was still there and he didn't want to jump. I asked him, "Will you go if I go?"

So I jumped out and he, Jeff was his name, came soon after.

As I floated down, I could see the plane going off in the distance. Below I could see a village and then a drainage ditch. As I got closer to the ground I could see I would hit the ditch, and actually I was lucky because it broke my fall.

It was now about one o'clock in the afternoon. Like all other airmen I was told to bury my chute, but I didn't have time for that. I immediately got out of the chute and started running for some woods. Then I could see some men running towards me so I took off in the other direction, but it was no use. I ran around a wire fence because I had a strange thought that it might have an electric charge. Soon after running around the fence the Germans caught up with me.

You know, during interrogation at Frankfurt the German interrogation officer asked me if we were using OBOE on the mission.

So I said, "What's that, a musical instrument?"

And he said, "Don't get smart with me. I can keep you here for months, or maybe even a year. They'll never know where you are. Come on, tell me. We're all in the same Air Force brotherhood anyway." What a bunch of garbage.

Now let me tell you more about that mission. The pilot and mid-upper were both killed when they went down with the plane. Whitaker, the second navigator, became a POW like myself and Jeff. The wireless-operator parachuted out, too, and I believe was a POW. The flight-engineer died when his chute opened and collapsed.

Bob Palmer, the OBOE leader on the mission, received the Victoria Cross posthumously. Two of his engines were on fire due to flak but he attacked regardless and dropped his bombs, then he hit the ground and that was it!

Overall, in our group of eight, none of us made it back to base. Five were shot down over Germany, two crashed in France and one crashed trying to get back to England, right on British soil.

Lancaster Comments

We thought it was the best heavy bomber in the whole war. It carried such a big bombload, but it still only needed a crew of seven. It also had speed and maneuverability which we all liked. I'll give you a good example of its speed by looking up an operation I did just before I was shot down.

On this operation, to Magdeburg, we left England with a tail wind of 50 knots and our speed was 258 knots; everything was done in knots and nautical miles. That's about 300 miles-per-hour with a wind of about 60. Coming back, after we dropped the bombs, we did 165 knots which is just under 200, and that's facing the same wind but with an empty bomb-bay.

FL W.E. Vaughan
RCAF
J24199

Life With The Belgian Underground

Pathfinding was a highly organized operation. I know, because I belonged to 405 Pathfinder Squadron. Our crew had to prove themselves with thirteen trips on Main Force with 427 Squadron before being 'invited' to a Pathfinder Squadron. Pathfinding was an elite group. They didn't just take anybody and you had to have experience as well as precision. You had to do your job well or you wouldn't be chosen. I'm sure there are many people out there who do not know the work we had to do. First of all I'll explain what Pathfinding was, without getting too technical, before I get into my favourite story.

To get the bombs dropped in the right place, the Main Force bombers needed an aiming-point. It was our job to drop ground-fire markers that the bombers could use to sight on and thereby hit the target. Let's say there were 1,000 bombers on a raid. They didn't just come over a city and dump all the bombs. They did it in waves and leading each wave were perhaps a dozen Pathfinders. The markers would only burn for about 3 minutes and that's why you needed Pathfinders for each wave. Once the markers hit the ground they produced very bright-coloured fires, sometimes green and other times red. Once the Germans caught onto our strategy they'd start some phoney fires to lead the Main Force away from the true aiming-point, but they never fooled anyone except the new crews. Our markers were much too bright to be mistaken for the German ones.

In each raid there was a Master Bomber who constantly circled the target-area and directed the Pathfinders by radio during the entire raid. He would talk to the Pathfinding Force but they were never allowed to talk to him. Radio silence was vital. He also made sure each set of ground markers were not creeping back. You see, many times the tendency was to drop the bombs just slightly before the aiming-point. As each bomber would do this, the next bomber in turn would drop his bombs, and before you knew it your aiming-point has crept back. The Master Bomber would then tell the next wave of Pathfinders to move up the markers by dropping them ahead of the actual aiming-point, so the process of creeping back would take longer. The Master Bomber had a dangerous job to perform. By always being over the target he was in constant danger from flak and fighters. I felt sorry for them. It was the worst job in all Bomber Command and had the highest casualty rate.

We did our Pathfinding on Lancasters. I was the radar navigator; bombing and map reading on the H2S. I would give a 'fix' to the regular navigator in longitude and latitude every 3 minutes. On a 3-hour trip, I'd give about sixty 'fixes'. This was done so that the bomber would never get off course. The navigator's job was to make sure he got the plane over the target. within 1 minute of the scheduled time.

On my twenty-eighth trip May 8, 1944 (fifty completed a tour of Pathfinding) we were sent to the Haine-St. Pierre marshalling yards in Belgium.

After we dropped our flares we were ordered to put our nose down and head straight for home; but we didn't make it back. We were alone in the sky and that's when it was easy to be tracked on the German ground-based radar. Before we knew it an Me-109 was coming up behind us. The wireless-operator picked him up on radar and notified the tail-gunner, but the tail-gunner then lost sight of the fighter. The pilot thought we should take evasive-action, but just as he started to move the Lancaster to one side we were hit. The German method after being guided to us by ground-based radar, was to sneak underneath us, point his fighter skyward, almost come to a stall and fire at the same time. That's how we got it. We ran right into the 109's cannon shells.

The two port engines and the port-wing tanks were in flames and the order to bail-out was given. The flight-engineer was supposed to go to the front hatch, rip off the emergency cover and jump out first. Then the rest of us would follow. He had his harness on but his leg straps weren't buckled up. So I went out headfirst and the rest followed; everybody except the tail-gunner who was killed by the 109.

Once I left the plane I waited for the usual count of ten. If you pulled the cord right when you left the plane you'd tear the chute to shreds. So you waited for your speed to slow down by counting to ten and then you pulled the cord. I counted and went to my right to grab the handle, but to my horror it wasn't there! Then I looked down to my left and it was there, thank God! A parachute fits two ways. So I pulled the handle and out came the chute.

I was floating down and the bright moonlight was lighting my way. Now I could see I faced a major problem: our own Lancasters were right above me and I might get hit! But as they came over I could see that I was a bit too low for them. As I descended further, I'd say about 9,000 feet by this time, I could see what I thought was France. But as I went lower I spotted a canal and I was heading straight for it, so I starting blowing up my Mae West life jacket. Then I tried to move the cords of the chute to one side to avoid hitting the canal. Canals had 6-foot high walls and if I landed in there I'd probably never get out. Adjusting the cords didn't seem to do any good, so I just left them. By now I faced another problem: I could see a forest beside the canal and that made me very nervous because I didn't want any sharp branches cutting through me!

It was a calm night with not a breath of wind. The ground was coming up very fast; almost too fast. My feet just grazed the top of some trees and I hit—and I mean hit!—the ground just beyond the forest in a cow pasture about 50 yards from the canal.

I hit the ground with a thud and the chute came down and neatly covered my body. The fall knocked me out because I fell backwards after my feet touched the ground. The first thing I did when I came to was bury my chute, just like they told us back in England. After that I checked for some cigarettes but couldn't find any.

The time was about 4 AM. What could I do? I was in enemy territory. The first thing I thought of was to walk to Spain, a neutral country, which was a mere 600 miles south, and from there get back to England. So, I started walking south. I decided I'd walk by night and hide by day, and maybe find a friendly house and get some food.

I went up one of the embankments along a canal and noticed a foot-path near the top. Then I thought I could walk the path during the day and get to a bridge or town. I was getting quite hungry and thirsty at this point. When I got to the top I became tired, so I laid down and fell asleep.

Sometime in the afternoon I was awakened by two young boys about 14 and 16 years old, who were staring at me. They must've known who I was because they probably heard the plane going down. I gave them some sign language to let them know what happened to me. They directed me to a cave at the side of the canal, then they let me know that someone would come for me at 11:30 that night.

Just before dark an old man came to my cave to give me something to eat. It was two slices of bread with something in the middle that tasted like axle-grease. Actually, rancid butter was more like it. The old man motioned on my watch that at 11:30 someone would be coming for me.

When the old man left, I left the cave and hid at another spot, but made sure that I could still see the cave. I wanted to make sure no Germans would be coming for me.

At 11:30 six men came and looked for me in the cave. When I could see that they weren't German soldiers, I came out and we all started talking. One of them gave me a bottle of beer which was my first drink of any kind in 34 hours. It was great! I could feel the moisture right down to my toes! But just then a farmer on a bicycle came and said a German patrol was coming our way. Everybody scattered except for myself and one other fellow. I guessed he was the one who was going to hide me.

We walked about two miles to his property and then he hid me in his tool shed. There I

Photo taken by Belgian underground, showing the remains of the Lancaster and the tail-gunner, F/Sgt Don Copeland. Note German soldiers around the wreckage, and the head of Raymonde Rocke in the foreground.

F/O Alex Nethery while in hiding. Taken by Raymonde Rocke's mother.

was, alone once again. The time was about 12:30 or 1 o'clock in the morning. I stayed in the shed a short while when I heard footsteps. My heart started thumping but, much to my relief it turned out to be the same fellow. I guess his wife gave him hell for leaving me in the shed and he came to get me and bring me into the house.

Inside, besides the family, were two big, fierce-looking black dogs. The farmer and his wife didn't know English and I didn't know much French, but we somehow got along because they had illustrated pictures around the room and by pointing and using sign language we managed to communicate.

We sat down and I was served coffee—the cup, I remember, didn't have a handle—and I was given a flat lump of sugar. I watched and noticed that they stuck the lump in their mouths and then took a sip of coffee, I did the same.

We were there until about 6 AM. They wanted me out of the house at that time because their kids would be waking up soon, and if they ever saw me they might blab around the school yard. So I was whisked out to some bushes until the kids left for school.

Shortly afterwards two people came to the house. They were from the Belgian underground and one of them was a lady, Raymonde Rocke, and she spoke some English. I now found out that I wasn't in France like I first thought, but was actually 5 miles inside Belgium!

By now I had replaced my Air Force clothes with civilian clothes and had been given a bike. Raymonde told me that she and her companion would bicycle along the canal foot-path, but I was to stay about a quarter mile behind so they wouldn't lose sight of me, or me of them, just in case a German patrol stopped me.

As we started I went only about 30 yards and the front tire blew, but I kept going with the tire flapping around the rim.

We went about 5 miles to a house near Raymonde's and I hid in a neighbour's garden until dark. Once the sun went down I went into Raymonde's house and when I got inside you'll never guess who was there! One of my crew members; George, the number one navigator. He made it, too, and he had cigarettes!

What a story George told me! I guess he went a little bonkers. After he had landed he took a benny tablet from his emergency kit and laid out in the sun and fell asleep, and got sunstroke. Then he walked right through a village in plain view of everybody, how he got past the Germans I'll never know, until an English lady who had married a local Belgian butcher noticed who he was and hauled him into her house.

Getting back to our situation there we were with Raymonde and her mother. Raymonde's father and brother had been shot by the Germans in the First World War, so there was no love lost for the Germans. I could see why she became a Belgian underground worker, even though the penalty for hiding any Allied airmen was death.

George and I hid there for four months. Remember, we were shot down on May 8, 1944. D-Day came a month later, and then it took three months for the American Army to liberate the area.

Their Army sure was a scruffy bunch. They had been advancing 40 or 50 miles a day and they didn't know where the heck they were since the right maps hadn't caught up with them yet. The night after the Americans arrived we spent the whole night with the American Commander, directing the rear-based Allied artillery by radio. Raymonde would get the results and new directions in French from the resistance fighters at the front and translate to the Commander in English.

I'd like to add something about the original raid and that is that three of the crew members landed in town when they parachuted out. Two of those landed right in the German barracks, so they were caught in about 30 seconds.

Lancaster Comments

What a beautiful aircraft! As a comparison between it and other bombers, it was like comparing a Lincoln to a Ford truck.

The Lancaster was a smooth and reliable machine. It could face a lot of battle damage and still go back for more. You'd just patch it up and send it out again.

It was quite fast considering the bomb-loads it carried and it seemed worthwhile to go on a raid with a Lancaster. Not so with a B-17 Flying Fortress. The B-17 was a well-armed aircraft, but there were so many good men killed on those American bombers and for a measily bomb-load of 4,000 pounds. The Lancaster could carry three times that.

F/O Alex Nethery
RCAF
J19356

A Prisoner in Poland

On July 26, 1942, my thirteenth mission and my wife's birthday, I was shot down over the North Sea. Our squadron, 158 RAF, had just come back from a bombing run to Hamburg and we had been using the flight commander's Halifax for the mission.

The Germans got a fix on us from their radar stations and predicted a Ju-88, a twin-engined fighter with airborne radar, onto us. It snuck up in front of us, got underneath and raked us with cannon fire. It all happened so fast, we never saw him coming.

I was the mid-upper gunner for that trip and I could see the German fighter after it flew past us, but by that time it was too late as we were already going down. Myself, the navigator and the tail-gunner managed to fall out just after the Halifax's petrol tanks exploded, and the aircraft came apart in mid-air at about 100 feet over the water. The other crew members didn't make it.

The three of us, once we hit the water, managed to float on one of the wings which had been turned up slightly with the tail flaps in the water. The petrol and air pockets in the wing tanks kept the wing on the water's surface. We never got to the dinghy because it was kept in the other wing and that wing had come apart during the explosion.

On the second day, when the weather was getting pretty rough, a German sea plane found us and dropped onto the water and let out a dinghy. A German, who was in the dinghy, got sick from the high waves as he tried to pull us in. That's how bad the weather had been, for about 30 hours after first hitting the water.

From there we were taken to a German Air Force base on Norderney Island, where we were put into some dry clothes. But it wasn't so easy getting the old ones off. The salt water had stuck my silk long johns right to my skin and to get them off they had to pluck me like a chicken. All the hair on my body came off with it.

Then we were taken to Dulag Luft in Frankfurt for interrogation. The fellow who handled the interrogation had been a fellow worker at the Grain Exchange in Winnipeg. He worked only two floors up and he even knew the people I had worked with. I couldn't believe it! I guess that's why he was in Canada back then to get information. We called them 'sleepers'. Germany had sent them over to North America during the 1930's to obtain all kinds of information, then recalled them just before the war started and put them into uniform. That's exactly what happened with this fellow.

At Frankfurt they took our Air Force clothes and gave us some old clothes. Then we were put in solitary with no windows or proper food, and there you'd stay locked up for a few weeks. After that many POW's were ready to tell anything. Other chaps were troublemakers and they got a beating, but most of us just gave our name, rank and serial number for the Red Cross to send word back home.

After the solitary we were put in cattle cars and we spent a four-day trip going to Stalag VIII-B in Lamsdorf, Poland, our POW camp. This same camp was used during the First World War for Allied prisoners. In fact, one Australian fellow with us spent a few years in it during that war. He ended up spending nine years there in total.

There were about 18,000 in our camp with 1,500 airmen in the centre compound, and 6,500 on work parties which were attached to the outside of the camp doing various jobs. The two outside compounds were Army men. They never let us airmen on the work parties because with our training in navigation we were considered a risk.

The POW barracks.

The 'forty-holer'.

Most of the German guards on these work parties were older men who were too old to fight. One time a guard went out with a small work crew but had a heart attack and died. The prisoners carried him back to camp with one prisoner carrying the gun. That sure caused an instant panic in the camp! German guards were running everywhere trying to decide what to do.

After we were at the camp a short time, we realized that the American Flying Fortresses were using our camp as some sort of navigation marker. They'd come up from Italy to bomb nearby centres and it seemed right when they were overheard, they'd make their turn. They were sure high up; they had to be 30,000 feet. All we could see were their vapour trails; you couldn't even see the outlines of the planes. Sometimes we'd see a Fortress get shot down. You'd see a puff of smoke, then see them go into a spin. We'd be on the ground and looking up. "Jump!" we'd cry out, and when we saw parachutes we felt a lot better.

By the end of 1944 the Russians were getting closer. By January, 1945 we were moved out, guards and all. The POW's were grouped, given Red Cross parcels and ordered to march. And march we did, for about three months. Some collapsed and were thrown into a cart with other bodies. Some guards dropped too, because they were marching right along with us.

Finally, when we were in Magdeburg, Germany, we were liberated by an American Army group and a day or so later we were all flown back to England on Dakotas. After three years I was going home!

Bomber Comments

The Wellington was a tough machine that could take a lot of battle damage and still come back on one engine. It wasn't the best bomber in the world but it was tough. I still remember the first time we had a 4,000-pound bomb aboard; it was so big that they had to take the bomb doors off and tuck the bomb part-way up the bomb-bay. When we let it go over the target, the Wellington flipped right over on its back!

The Halifax was an even bigger change for me because it was so big and fast. The tail-gunners loved it because they were given an almost endless supply of bullets along the conveyor system. The smaller bombers kept the bullets in their turrets and when they ran out, too bad!

When we carried the 8,000 pound bombs, two 4,000-pound bombs connected, crew members had to steady the bomb doors as they were being closed over the bombs, otherwise you might scrape a bomb or two and then...Every crew member hated that job.

WO$_1$ Al Bridgwater
RCAF
R65731

Wellington over enemy territory

A Machine Gun for 1,500 Cigarettes

It was the dream of everyone on Bomber Command to get into Pathfinders. These aircraft (in this case the Halifax) carried green or red target indicators which would light up the target for Bomber Command.

After an advanced training course in radar we were posted to 35 Pathfinder Squadron at Gravely, just south of Cambridge. This was another typical Royal Air Force squadron and they did not like anybody to abort an operation. We signed on for 50 operations. A tour on Bomber Command was thirty operations and you expected to serve two of those after which you could do what you liked, but because of the high risk in Pathfinders we were given one tour of 50 operations.

On the night of December 4, 1943 our target was Leipzig, Germany. Our radar was not operating properly and we were the first aircraft over the Dutch coast. Furthermore, we were 8 miles north of Track which meant we were sticking out like a sore thumb. We just got over the Dutch coast when the German flak shot out our starboard-inner engine. It began to flame and shortly after a German fighter came in underneath and shot out the starboard-outer engine. By this time the whole aircraft was on fire and we had to jump.

Three of us got out and three were trapped in the aircraft. My navigator, the seventh man in the crew, panicked and pulled his chute in the aircraft and fell to his death. I landed in the Zuider Zee and there was ice floating around me. I was only 100 yards from the shore but had extreme difficulty with my parachute cords. I finally collapsed unconscious on the shore after about one-half hour. I woke 5 hours later and found that I had been captured by the Germans.

The Germans threw us into a jail in Amsterdam, Holland. Every week they would take a trainload of shot-down prisoners down the Ruhr. I won't forget that trip. We travelled from nine in the morning till two or three in the afternoon, remember this was the industrial centre of Germany and very heavily populated. During the whole trip we were looking out the windows and we never saw an undamaged house.

We finally finished up in Frankfurt, which was the largest rail depot in Germany. It had twenty-six loading platforms and tracks headed for all parts of Europe. Suddenly our guard announced that we would have to stay in the station overnight and leave in the morning. This was the worst night I ever spent in my life. Pathfinders were advised in advance of future targets in Germany and I knew that Frankfurt was next on the list. At that moment the air raid sirens went on! However, because of the atmospheric conditions they bypassed us and went on to another target. This was my most terrifying experience in the war.

The next morning we pushed on a short distance to the famous Interrogation Centre in Frankfurt: Dulag Luft. We were then placed in solitary confinement for periods of up to fourteen days. This treatment was reserved for officers only, as they figured we had more information. I remember a fake Red Cross man who wore a red band on his arm with the famous cross. He wanted to know my squadron and other information so that he could advise my next of kin. This was utter bull! I gave him my name, rank and serial number which was all we were permitted to give.

The accommodations were wooden barracks with very little insulation and for a week the Germans gave us the hot and cold treatment. From outside your cell they could turn your heat on and the temperature could rapidly go up to 85 or 90 degrees. About 3 hours later they would turn it off and the temperature would drop to 35 or 40 degrees. The rationale here was that the rapid changes in temperature would break down your resistance to questions.

During the second week we were subjected to interrogations by German officers at between one and three in the morning. These interrogators had an amazing amount of detail about our squadron, including names and plans. Of course the attempt again was to deliberately disconcert you so as to jog out another piece to their jigsaw puzzle.

My final interview with the interrogation officer was rather amusing. He had a well-appointed office including tapestries all over. As I entered the office I noticed with surprise that he had a luger pistol on the right-hand side of his desk. He started interrogating me in a rather aggressive fashion: intimating that if I did not answer he would shoot me in my chair!

I laughed outright. The idea that he would haul out a gun and get blood all over his carpets and walls was ludicrous. If he was serious, of course, all he had to do was call in a squad of soldiers to take me out in the yard and shoot me.

In his summation he told me that my lack of knowledge about aircraft matters was absolutely staggering and if I were a member of the German Air Force I would not be allowed to hold a commission. The next day I was shipped out to a proper prison camp, much to my relief.

I was posted to Stalag Luft Barth 1, which was located between Rostock and Lubeck on the coast of the Baltic. This was perhaps one of the most humane POW camps in Germany, as we had an Austrian commanding officer who was obviously anti-Nazi. Let me point out that our conditions were far better than those of concentration camps which were reserved for Jews and political prisoners. Next to being a prisoner-of-war, the worst job I can imagine is being a prisoner-of-war guard. They were old men, some of them convalescing from war wounds and if they did not abide by the German regulations, their supreme punishment was to be sent to the Eastern Front in Russia. As you may have read, the Germans felt a strange sort of sympathy towards us and had a fantasy that together with the British, they could both fight the Russians, whom they feared.

The prison camp was well situated on a sandy coast. We were constantly digging tunnels but we could not go down more than 4 feet because sea water would start to creep in. This meant that we had to continually shore them up with bedboards. Eventually none of us had any bedboards left. We therefore resorted to stealing wire since our bunks were double and we had to reinforce them somehow.

The Germans, with their heavy sense of humour, put up a cross in memory of the 108th tunnel; but we bothered them night and day. As Canadians we received thousands of cigarettes from Canada, unlike the British and Americans. These became a currency with which you could bribe the Germans. They were using artificial tobacco and one cigarette was worth 4 Deutsche marks, or roughly a dollar in Berlin money. At one time they offered to sell us a machine gun for 1,500 cigarettes.

Internally, the camp was controlled by the prisoners through the senior commanding officer. He in turn was supported by the XYZ committee who controlled things like the planning of escapes, uniforms, clothing, and false documents. Many of the parcels sent from overseas to the prisoners were channelled through intelligence and furnished with escape aids such as hack-saw blades and radio parts.

We had a lot of talent in the prison camp. They were continually entertaining us with music and plays which were current in that year. The most famous one was 'Front Page'. Even the German officers used to come in and sit down and applaud wildly at our plays.

Naturally the XYZ committee was reading and approving our constant plans of escape. Sometimes an escape meant going into hiding and pretending that you had escaped. One day the Germans found out at the morning roll call that three of the members were missing. Their procedure was to line us up in front of our barrack blocks and as they'd call out our names they would look at our card with the photograph on it and by process of elimination know who the three men were. Sometimes we'd be out for 4 or 5 hours. All the time the Germans were particularly terrified of the Gestapo and they did everything in their power to keep them away. However, once a prisoner escaped the Gestapo would move in and do a personal search of everyone in the block. This was done on the parade ground which was roughly one-half mile square and also very sandy.

As we were being checked out one of the prisoners yelled at the German guard. As the guard turned his face away, another prisoner picked up roughly 100 identification cards (complete with photograph and odd bits of information), whip into the barrack block and threw them into the fire. By this time the Germans were going crazy, and threatened to shoot us all! The camp had been extended to the point where we now numbered about 15,000.

The Germans, with their tracking dogs, came in and ripped out the boards in our sleeping quarters and searched the place for the missing cards. Naturally they found nothing. Out on the parade ground they announced there would be a body search, so we all sat down in the sand, piled up little mounds and stuck a piece of paper or wooden stick in each one. The Germans, ever methodical, brought in about 100 guards and proceeded to rake the whole area in their attempt to find the missing documents. In our assessment, this was a very successful maneuver on our part, as it kept the guards on a 24-hour alert.

During the first six months of imprisonment we received Red Cross parcels from England, Canada and the States. This, coupled with the meager ration which the Germans offered, was sufficient to keep us going.

During the last twelve months, however, the Allies were using long-range fuel tanks which enabled their fighter aircraft to penetrate right into Berlin. They shot at every rail movement and as a result German trains could not get through to us. However, about a week before the war ended we received a new shipment of parcels which had many dummy 20mm shells. The doctor got on the loud speaker system and asked us to avoid eating heavily, but that night three people died from overeating.

There was no stealing in the prison camp. In roll-call the Germans would call us out and people would leave things like watches and rings on the table, and the Germans did not dare take them for fear they would be picked up and sent to the Eastern Front. We had one German guard who was a real ulcer. We planted him with a package of American cigarettes and when he got to the gate we yelled, "SPY! SPY!" He was searched, the cigarettes were found on him and he was promptly sent to Russia as punishment.

One morning we woke up to find that the German guards were gone. The Russians had surrounded us but we were not allowed to move out of the camp. I did get a chance to visit the local concentration camp. This was modelled after the Royal Air Force aerodrome, and I found out later that the Germans prided themselves on copying English techniques.

In May of 1945 we realized that our next enemies were going to be the Russians. It took a week of negotiating with them to fly us out of Germany.

I was flown home to the Ford Aerodrome in England late in May of 1945. This was a wonderful experience and although we had no money, the English people were so grateful that they constantly gave us meals and beer. The only thing I brought home from Germany was a German parachute. Silk was highly prized in those days.

In the first week in June, 1945, I boarded a ship and sailed for Canada.

Halifax Comments

A wonderful aircraft with some excellent equipment. Although it came second-best to the Lancaster, the Halifax could take a lot more punishment. It would get all shot full of holes and still make it back to England.

The crew comforts were great. I read somewhere that it was a cold plane. That's a bunch of garbage. Heck, I never froze in the thing. Even the tail-section, which was the coldest part of any bomber, wasn't all that bad.

F/L Jack Bonet
RCAF
J20043

F/L Jack Bonet, on the right, with two friends in London, in May or June of 1943.

Crew of the Superstitious Aloysious at Chakulia Air Base, India, December, 1944.

Standing (l to r): Major George T. Weschler—pilot and aircraft commander; Sgt Wnuk, gunner; Sgt Swanson, Central Fire Control, which is top gunner; Sgt. Gehrig, gunner; Sgt Jarman, gunner. Kneeling: Lt Fred Wolkoff, radar; Capt Clark Thomas, navigator; Lt Shelly Green, co-pilot; Lt James O'Keefe, bombardier; Lt Edwin Mann, flight-engineer.

'The Superfortress'
—the B-29 against the Japanese

Flak and Searchlights

It was on one of the Mukden missions in December, 1944. I flew as bombardier on Major Weschler's crew and our plane was the *Superstitious Aloysious*, a B-29 Superfortress.

The target was to be hit at about 10 AM which meant a take-off time of about 3 AM. Sunrise would come around 7 AM. In the middle of the night we gathered in the briefing room to hear Lou Scherck describe the target, our routes out and home, and areas to be avoided. Lou then closed the briefing as he always did by admonishing us to wear our GI shoes, in the event we were forced to bail out and do some walking.

Clark Thomas was our navigator and an excellent one. But during the three hours between 3 AM and 6 AM he had to rely entirely upon celestial navigation, and no matter how fast you plotted them, you were always 50-70 miles off the plane's location.

Around 6 AM the sky had lightened to the point where it was difficult to shoot any stars with the octant and the ground was still in darkness. Clark went over to Dead Reckoning. The winds over northern China blow in mysterious ways.

As bombardier I did as much pilotage as possible to help the navigator. When the ground became visible I reached for my maps, and at that moment I looked ahead and made out the outlines of a city. Several miles to the north of it I saw a large river which could be none other than the Yellow River. I quickly checked the map then announced over the intercom that we were coming up on Kaifeng.

I remembered from some reading which I had done on China's history, that Kaifeng was one of the oldest cities. At one time it was the eastern terminus of the Old Silk Road, one of the longest and greatest of Asian trade routes. In centuries past, caravans leaving Kaifeng had gone to the shores of the Black Sea. How exciting, I thought, to fly low at about 4,000 feet over this historic city and to see its ancient walls and buildings gleaming gold in the first light of the sun. Little columns of smoke were rising from chimneys all over the city as people stirred about and prepared the morning meals. Others, leading pack animals, were moving on the roads leading to the city. I saw railroad lines coming from the east, checked them against the map, and as we came over the city I stated, "This is definitely Kaifeng." Outside of an acknowledgement from Clark, I don't recall that anyone said anything. I'm sure that all were looking down marvelling at the sights of the awakening city.

At about that time there appeared over my head, as they appeared in cartoons, a light bulb which suddenly switched on. I reached into my bombardier kit, pulled out the briefing notes and read to myself, "Kaifeng, heavily defended headquarters of the Japanese Army in Honan Province. Avoid."

It was a bit too late to avoid, as we were sailing majestically over the center of town, our silver wings and fuselage gleaming brightly! Any second now, I thought, every anti-aircraft gun in and around the city will fire simultaneously, and the *Superstitious Aloysious* will disintegrate into scrap aluminum. But to the best of my recollection not a single shot was fired and we flew on to Manchuria.

*   *   *   *   *

"Now what?" we all wondered as we filed in to hear a special critique and briefing. A number of us were still shaking from the last mission of May 24, 1945, when the anti-aircraft guns and night-fighters in and around Tokyo had inflicted heavy losses on the B-29's. Shaking also from what we had seen of the hell created by our incendiary bombs that night. We were to go back to that city almost immediately and the crews who were scheduled for the mission were not envied by the others.

Strange sightings had been reported to the intelligence officers at the interrogations following the May 24 mission. Discounting over-wrought imaginations and the tricks which night shadows play on the vision, there was still evidence that something new and ominous in the way of a night fighter had been present in the skies over Tokyo in the early morning hours. We could account for many of our lost planes for they had been seen going down. But some had disappeared without a trace. Over the target several blinding explosions, many times greater than ordinary flak bursts, had been observed and we now suspected that the planes unaccounted for had vanished in them.

Our intelligence officers sorted through the interrogation reports and found details of a crude, small aircraft captured by the marines on Okinawa and radio messages broadcast by raving Japanese military leaders. As early as February, 1944, one of them had said, "We are now in a situation where we can demand nothing better than crash tactics, which ensure the destruction of an enemy plane at one fell swoop, thus striking terror into his heart and rendering his powerfully armed and well-equipped airplanes useless." They came up with the Baka Bomb; a suicide plane which could be launched from the belly of a bomber such as the Betty, a standard Japanese medium bomber. Aside from the demented pilot, the plane carried a warhead weighing close to a ton, rocket fuel sufficient to keep the plane airborne for half an hour, and a rising sun flag presumably to be waved exultantly in the last few seconds before the explosion would atomize the Baka, its pilot, and its unfortunate target.

"The Baka Bomb can be aimed and released at you when you're caught in and illuminated by ground searchlight. But before you come in range of those searchlights beware of the mother plane which we think also carries a powerful searchlight capable of picking you up at a distance. And, of course, if the mother plane is one of the fast Bettys it can keep up with you, hold you in its light while its Baka is released and overtakes you. And...uh," the intelligence officer's voice trailed away. "You're welcome to look at these diagrams and pictures of this new weapon."

What we wanted from him, as he knew, was the means of dealing with a suicide attack. The appalling losses suffered by our Navy off Okinawa were known to us. Also known was the fact that the losses were due primarily to Kamikaze attack. But there were no satisfactory tactics that he or anyone could devise for us and we had no new, ingenious weapons that could neutralize the Bakas. Like the Navy, we would have to stand up to them, fight back with our present armament and hope that at their present stage of development the new suicide craft would be clumsy and crude enough so that we could evade them.

The following evening we took off, once more heading for Tokyo with the diagrams and pictures of the crude, but deadly, Baka vivid in our minds.

Hours later, in the early morning, we crossed the Japanese coastline, a landfall that always set the nerves on edge. Wheeling past Mt. Fujiyama, easily visible at night, we picked up the initial point and began the forty mile run to Tokyo. An alert, thinking enemy had seen only too well the advantages to us of this upwind approach, and had lined it with searchlights and anti-aircraft weapons of all kinds. Given the range and fury of the people below us, I could even picture slingshot brigades preparing to loose rocks at us.

One of our gunners now went to the rear hatch with sacks of 'window' metallic strips, which when thrown out would drift slowly downward and cloud up the radar scopes with which the searchlight crews and anti-aircraft gunners would try to track us. Searchlights picked us up immediately, and out the hatch went the 'window'. Bricks thrown at the searchlights would have been more useful. Radar was not needed to spot us on such a clear night and once the lights caught us, they clung to us tenaciously. With maddening precision and skill, each searchlight crew passed us on to the next light on the run.

Now the guns opened up! At an altitude of 9,000 feet we were in range of medium and light anti-aircraft weapons, as well as the heavy guns. The plane shook from direct hits. Before we reached the city, shells took out one engine, aerated both wings, set fire to the incendiary bombs in both bomb-bays, and punctured and shredded so many parts that only by prayer and luck did we stay airborne. It was a miracle that not one of us was scratched.

The minutes, always long on a bomb run, dragged and dragged. Finally we staggered over the city where rising smoke obscured us from the infuriating searchlights. The final seconds of the bomb run ticked off, then the bombs went away to add to the inferno and horror below us. Thermal updrafts now tossed us violently. Rod Wriston, as cool and able a pilot as ever I flew with, banked the battered plane slowly and carefully away from the burning city, the searchlights and the anti-aircraft guns. We caught our collective breaths only to grasp in sudden shock and alarm at the bright light which appeared above and in front of us. A mother plane's searchlight probing for us? And then below us a stream of tracers shot into the darkness, a B-29 gunner at what unknown menace?

I swung my gunsight to cover the light and brought four .50-calibre machine guns to bear on it. We staggered on, the light neither gaining on us nor fading away. We banked again and this brought us onto a south heading, the way to our base at Tinian. The great bright light was now to the east of us and it stayed there and was visible until the sun came up. It had actually been out there in space a few million years, sometimes appearing in the evening sky, sometimes in the morning sky. To us earthlings, studying the skies, Venus is by far and away the brightest and most brilliant of our neighbour planets.

There was yet another miracle that morning; our plane held together all the way home to Tinian. Rod landed it gently and with tenderness, but while taxiing to our hardstand it seemed to sigh with weariness and hurt, then it shuddered and collapsed. It never flew again.

At interrogation we had many things to report. Our own experiences, shaking as they had been, were as nothing compared to the fates of other crews. Stricken, burning B-29's had been seen plunging to earth all along that fearful run from the initial point to the city. Cruelest and most sickening of all sights that night was the B-29 with one engine on fire which had been turned into flaming wreckage by the guns of hysterical gunners on another B-29.

We left the interrogation room and sought out our cots. Sleep did not come to me. Struggling to put the horrors of the mission out of my mind, I turned to humour, the counterpoise that preserves sanity.

I had not reported the Great Searchlight in the Sky, but rumors had circulated over at interrogation. Several gunners and bombardiers on other crews had seen the light and fired on it without hesitation. The .50-calibre slugs, directed by the marvellously precise electronic sight, had sped unerringly toward the target.

I got up and poked through my footlocker and found some notes from navigation school. The target was about 26 million miles away. Given the muzzle velocity, a little acceleration beyond the earth's atmosphere and the distance to travel, the slugs should've landed on Venus about twelve months later.

Superfortress Comments

In my opinion, the bombardier had a good station in the '29. You were not isolated from the pilot as you were in the B-17 and the B-24. Even if the intercom failed you had instant communication with the pilot, and always knew what was going on up on the flight deck.

I also liked the firepower at our station, the bombardier also acted as nose-gunner. We had control of four .50-calibre machine guns in the upper turret and two 50's in the lower turret. So the firepower against head-on attacks was formidable.

We had problems in the beginning with general maintenance and performance. Our Group, the 40th, was one of four which formed the 58th Wing. The 58th Wing took the first B-29's into combat and the problems with the new, untried plane were severe.

1st/Lt James J. O'Keefe
USAAF
0-746740

Raid Over Kobe

I was a pilot with the 25th Bombardment Squadron, 40th Bombardment Group (Very Heavy) of the United States Army Air Forces. My combat missions first started out of our base at Chakulia, India. January 2, 1945 was our first mission and our craft was a B-29 Superfortress which we called the *Rankless Wreck*, a plane reputed to have had the distinction of never completing a mission.

A few months later our squadron and group moved to Tinian Island, where we flew several raids on the Japanese homeland. Three noteworthy missions for us happened in the months of May and June. All three were incendiary raids on Japanese cities.

On the 24th of May we hit at the heart of Japan, Tokyo, on the first of our night missions. The first mission was relatively uneventful but when we came the second time, a few days later, they were ready for us.

It was May 26. Our altitude was only about 10,000 feet and when we went over Tokyo the searchlights were everywhere. We went in single file and we could look out over the yellow-flamed sky and see the other B-29's stretched out on our right and left. Our plane was quite fortunate not to be caught in any searchlights on both Tokyo raids. But every now and then we would see a B-29 picked up in the cone of the lights and after that would catch hell from the anti-aircraft fire below.

On this particular night we were one of the last going through and we were caught in the middle of the fire storm. Our plane moved into the smoke clouds that were created by the incendiary bombs. Our plane was blown from this altitude of 10,000 feet to an altitude of 15,000 feet in just a matter of seconds! We ended up on our side and every red light on the aircraft came on! Then we went into a dive where we approached speeds of 500 miles-per-hour. We finally levelled it out with very little altitude to spare. We just couldn't believe the power of that fire storm. We were tossed like a leaf in a wind storm.

I remember too, on that raid, the stench of the wood burning below us. The whole city in flame was as light as day; just an unbelievable scene below. Some of the other planes which were tossed about from the fire winds didn't recover and we lost them.

On May 29th we made another fire-bomb raid, a daylight one on Yokohama. We flew over at around 16,000 feet and I remember that the bombing was so extensive that we didn't go back again.

The No. 3 plane in our formation, we were No. 1, which was the plane on our right was rammed in the back by one of the Japanese fighters! This was a horrible experience for our crew to see, especially the gunners, right off our wing. I don't think our gunners completely recovered from that for the balance of our missions.

Also, over Yokohama we were bombed from the air by the Japanese. They were phosphorous bombs from above. Fortunately for us, they didn't hit one aircraft. I remember, too, the flak. It was so close that we could hear the bursts and see the orange flame. By this time the Japanese concentrated on putting some of their best flak gunners in Tokyo and the Yokohama area. Yokohama was the largest Japanese naval base and the gunners there knew what they were doing.

The *Rankless Wreck* flew its last mission on June 5, a raid on Kobe.

We flew over Kobe at about 14,000 feet. The crew was the same except we had a new bombardier aboard, his first flight. The anti-aircraft fire over Kobe was spectacular. There were ships in the harbour shooting away at us. We were flying the high slot, No. 4, in the right-hand flight off the lead flight. A George fighter in a gentle circle out a couple of miles ahead was at 1 o'clock and slightly below the formation. With our bomb-bay doors open on the bomb run and just as our bombs went away the George pilot made his move. He headed straight for us and at about 200 yards fired both his 40mm cannons, snap-rolled over on his back and dove straight down, passing under us. All the while our rookie bombardier, transfixed, stared in awe and pointed at the fighter. He shouted, "Look at him come!"

"Look at him, hell", I said, "Shoot! Shoot!" By this time the waist gunners were blasting

The crippled 'Rankless Wreck' limps toward Iwo Jima, June 5th, 1945, as seen through the cockpit of the escorting B-29.

away at him but I don't believe they touched him. One of the shells hit the left outboard engine and it went out immediately in a bath of oil and smoke, so we feathered the prop. Another shell struck the fuselage just behind the bulkhead where the radio operator sat and exploded inside the bomb-bay, destroying the electrical system, the hydraulic system and leaving one of the bomb-bay doors dangling and unable to be cranked shut. Lucky for us we were hit about 20 seconds after we dropped our bombs. With all of the electrical systems out we had no turbo-chargers operating on our three remaining engines and they were now delivering one-third less power.

In our stricken condition we had quickly slowed down and the rest of the formation moved away. In a few moments we looked around and one of our B-29 buddies had come up on our right wing, slowing down to stay with us. He saw our trouble and decided to help out.

Together we headed south over Japan toward the sea. We were under attack a couple of times by fighters but our buddy managed to fight them off without further damage to our plane.

Our central fire control officer came forward to the bomb-bay, closed the doors which were still operable, then attempted to repair our damaged electrical system. He burned his hands in the process and had no success.

Soon we were out over the water flying on three engines and no turbo-chargers. Our airspeed was down to about 160. Our props were turning so slowly you could almost watch them. Then we spotted Iwo Jima. Iwo had a short gravel-covered fighter strip only 2000 feet long. We cranked down our landing gear, gave the *Rankless Wreck* about 15 degrees of flap and landed on the gravel. With no brakes to slow our 29 we quickly ran out of runway. Our speed was still around 95-miles-per-hour. The plane, lurching and staggering, finally was slowed to a stop by the many shell holes and pot holes and ended up sitting at a right angle to the direction of the runway. Everybody scrambled like crazy to get out of the plane, fearing an explosion. Not one of us had a scratch.

I ran about 100 feet, then I stopped and my knees buckled under me from the fright of it all. Our tail-gunner reacted differently. He ran and couldn't stop until someone finally caught up with him and slowed him down.

All of us were taken to the Iwo hospital and released after the medics determined we were all right. That night we were flown back to our base at Tinian.

We later found out that the *Rankless Wreck* had 148 holes in the bomb-bay. It was the end of the line for our plane but it had served us well. Prior to our crew taking the *Rankless Wreck* it had never completed a mission. After a long haul against the Japanese, Kobe was its last run.

Superfortress Comments

Because the B-29 was rushed into production, many problems became apparent during the first couple years of its existence. The Wright engines were sometimes nicknamed 'Wrong' engines or 'Flamethrowers'. They'd conk out or catch fire in the air. They'd overheat constantly, cylinder heads would blow off and they also acquired many oil leaks. In India the engines even ran too hot on the ground. But by November, 1944, the Superfortresses that came to India for combat against the Japanese were of much better quality than previous ones.

The first time I saw a B-29 up close I couldn't believe something that big could actually get off the ground and fly. Structurally they were very strong. They could withstand fire storms over Japan as well as any fierce thunderstorms we encountered. It was this ruggedness that got us home from our missions.

No plane that the USAAF made was more challenging or exciting to fly. We hated it on occasion but loved it most of the time. It was completely efficient with no wasted space anywhere.

The visibility was great, due to the plexiglass nose. One pilot once said, "Flying the B-29 was like flying a 3-bedroom house from the front porch."

As time progressed we had more and more respect for the Superfortress. Its only shortcoming was that it was needed before it was ready.

Capt. J. Ivan Potts, Jr.
USAAF
0449381

The mighty Superfortress

'Fighters'
—stories from fighter pilots

Landing at Normandy

I flew with a Typhoon fighter unit; 193 RAF Squadron. Our base of operations was at Harrowbeer near Yelverton, South Devon, England, about 8 miles north of Plymouth. The Squadron formed in late December, 1943.

From Harrowbeer we moved up to a number of different bases along the south coast of England and early in 1944 became part of the 2nd Tactical Air Force.

Our first operations were coastal patrols to counteract the fighter-bomber raids by the Focke-Wulf 190 on the towns along the south coast of England. We also did shipping recces where we looked for targets along the north coast of Brittany, in France.

Also, we carried out what were called Rangers. They were wide-ranging attacks on enemy airfields and trains in northern France. Once we became a bomber unit, we attacked flying-bomb sites, radar stations, marshalling yards and bridges along the Seine in preparation for D-Day in Normandy.

After D-Day we became a close support unit for the Canadian Army in the Northwest European Campaign. We attacked tank formations, ammunition dumps, troop concentrations and enemy headquarter units.

I well remember what the D-Day operation looked like from the air. The day our Wing Commander led our unit on a recce behind the beachhead in Normandy.

On the way over we saw the incredible sight of a solid line of ships stretching from England to France. Just off the French coast was a formation of the largest battleships in the world, and they were firing shells inland. The whole thing was really impressive.

On the road west of Caen we spotted two enemy tanks which we first dive-bombed, then attacked from all directions with our cannon fire. Later, when we viewed the combat films, I saw my own aircraft pass through the target area of one of the other aircraft taking part in it.

One of the most satisfying missions I was on was the closing of a tunnel in which a long-range enemy gun was stored. The Germans would take this gun out at night and shell the beach-head. Intelligence learned from the French underground where the gun was kept and six of us went over, three planes on each end of the tunnel, and with two 1,000-pound bombs aboard our Typhoons we skip-bombed the mouths of the tunnel.

Skip-bombing was carried out by flying in a shallow dive, almost to ground level, then releasing the bombs which skipped along the ground and entered the mouth of the tunnel, closing it up. Bombs that were used on low-level attacks had 10-second delayed-action fuses which allowed the aircraft to clear the area. There was a bit of flak from the guns above the tunnel mouth which damaged one of the aircraft but we all returned home safely.

As a fighter-bomber pilot I saw very few enemy aircraft. But on June 29, 1944, I saw more than I wanted to see at one time.

Our Wing Leader who went on that trip, Johnny Baldwin, had built up an impressive total of enemy aircraft destroyed, about fifteen at that point. He had been the CO on other Typhoon fighter squadrons which had run into many Me-109's and Focke-Wulf 190's.

On this particular trip we were carrying out an armed recce west of Paris. Three sections of four aircraft took off from England but two aircraft had to return because of engine trouble.

193 RAF Fighter-Bomber Squadron in front of a Typhoon at Normandy, July, 1944. Jack Brown is sitting in the first row directly behind the nose of the bomb.

We were equipped with long-range tanks to allow us a greater radius of action. Over France there was 10-10ths cloud at 7,500 feet and we were travelling east near Evreux, when ahead and to our left below we saw about twenty or thirty Me-109's and they were heading in our direction. We immediately jettisoned the long-range tanks and switched on the gun sight and firing button on the control column.

I was flying No. 3 to the Wing Commander, whose section was the closest to the 109's. As I turned toward the 109's I opened fire and pulled the nose of the aircraft past the line of enemy planes. I didn't see how I could miss. Then, to avoid a collision I pulled into a tight turn and kept turning to avoid becoming a sitting target. As I completed 360 degrees, the 109's were climbing away ahead of me. When I looked around I saw three 109's behind me ready to open fire! I pulled into a tight, climbing turn in an attempt to reach the safety of the cloud layer above. Looking around I saw spurts of flames shooting out of the cannons of the 109's, just as you'd see in a movie, only this was for real and I was the target!

Suddenly there was a bright flash and a loud bang, as a cannon shell burst above my engine. As I pulled the turn tighter, the Typhoon lost flying speed and started to spin. I remember thinking, "This is it!" I recalled that we once were told that if we ever got into a spin below 7,500 feet we wouldn't have enough height to pull out. The next thing I knew the aircraft was diving straight for the deck, but fortunately for me I was heading north toward the French coast. I noticed several 109's were still following me, so I waited till the last moment before levelling off just above the tree tops. As I did so, I saw one of the 109's behind me crash to the deck in flames! He was either concentrating too much on getting me into his sights or his plane wouldn't pull out of the dive.

It's amazing how efficiently your mind operates when your life is on the line. I suddenly recalled a combat report that I had read a year before on how a Spitfire pilot caught up to a 109 he was chasing because the 109 kept jinking to avoid being hit, and thus lost flying speed. I was determined I wasn't going to get caught in the same way, so I relied on the 'Tiffie's' speed to get away in a straight line. I hugged the tree tops and as I crossed the Seine, a few miles east of Le Havre, I went down one bank and up the other, narrowly missing hydro wires on the other side. Once I reached the French coast, the enemy gave up the chase.

Typhoon 1B with three-bladed prop and 'car door' type cockpit enclosure.

As I throttled back, the engine began to vibrate. I headed for the line of ships which stretched four abreast from England to Normandy. I was prepared to bail out near the ships if I had to, but I thought I should at least attempt a landing on one of the advanced landing strips near the beach-head, which I ended up doing without much difficulty.

After landing, the ground crews advised me that both the magnetos were damaged and there was a 3-inch hole in each of the opposite blades of the 4-bladed prop.

I left my aircraft there and returned to England in a Transport Command Anson. When I reached base, I heard that another pilot had been forced to land in Normandy because he too had been shot up. I also heard that seven Me-109's had been destroyed and two damaged.

Typhoon Comments

The specs on it were that it was armed with four 20mm cannons, and could carry up to 2,000 pounds of bombs or eight 60-pound rockets. The engine was a 24-cylinder Napier Sabre which generated over 2,000 horsepower. The aircraft, when loaded, weighed about 7 tons.

The Typhoon was designed to be a replacement for the Hurricane and Spitfire but production was rushed when the Focke-Wulf 190 came on the scene. Because it was put into service too soon, the Typhoon had many problems. Performance at high altitude wasn't the best, tails fell off because of elevator problems, engines seized and some pilots were asphyxiated from the engine fumes. Most of the problems were eventually solved and later on the Typhoon proved to be an excellent machine of close support and fighter-bomber work.

I personally found it an exceptionally rugged machine which could take a great deal of punishment from flak, enemy aircraft and contact with ground objects. It was steady in a dive and very maneuverable for its size and weight. Apart from an oil line failure and a few starting problems, I had no difficulties with it. It was a delight to fly.

F/L Jack Brown
RCAF
J17853

I Can't Feel My Nose

I graduated in the cadet class of 43A as a single-engine pilot at Craig Field, Selma, Alabama in January of 1943. My first training in tactical aircraft was at Key Field, Meridian, Mississippi in A-24 dive-bombers, otherwise known as the SBD or Douglas Dauntless. This took place from February until April when a number of us were sent to Harding Field, Baton Rouge, Louisiana for more training in the relatively new A-36A, the dive-bomber version of the P-51; so called because it had been designed with dive-brakes to hold the terminal velocity in a dive to approximately 375 mph. Like the P-51, this model grew to be much loved by its pilots. When most of us got sent overseas in August we had at least 100 hours of tactical training in it.

Many of us ended up in the 12th Air Force in Italy, in either the 27th or the 86th Fighter-Bomber Group. I was in the 525th Squadron of the latter. I flew combat missions from October until July of 1944, during which time I had also checked out in P-40's and the twin-engined UC-78 which was used to transport VIP's to Anzio from Naples. I left Corsica just at the time our group began operating P-47's, so I never got to fly the Jug in combat.

In September, back in the States, I got assigned to a tactical support group flying P-40's from DeRidder, Louisiana, moving with it up to Stuttgart, Arkansas in February, 1945.

At Stuttgart we flew relatively new P-40's until June, when we received brand new P-51D's. My transition to these shiny steeds was relatively easy because of all my previous P-51 and A-36A time. Perhaps I was over-confident although I prefer not to think so. I any case, I logged 19 hours in June, 21 hours in July and 18 hours in August, all in the Mustang. On the 18th of August, the fateful day, I logged five minutes!

As pilots we were supposed to make at least one 1,000 mile cross-country flight each month, either on a tactical mission or on an R & R trip on a weekend. I had decided to spend the weekend at the Georgia Military Academy in College Park near Atlanta, two and one-half hours away as I recall. When we had a long flight scheduled such as this, the crew chief would fill all tanks including the fuselage tank behind the cockpit which held about 85 gallons. This tank had recently been restricted to holding 15 gallons for tactical operations because some pilots had gotten into deep trouble and sometimes fatal accidents, by doing aerobatics with the tank full.

I'm not sure whether it was according to or against regulations for operating procedures, but we normally took off with the 'ON' tank selector switch on the fuselage tank for a cross-country flight in order to burn off the fuel as soon as possible. After this tank was close to empty we would be ready for any unusual maneuver or a dogfight. I performed my cockpit check in the normal manner and could have sworn I saw the gauge on the rear tank reading 'full'. Also, the crew chief had given the aircraft its preflight that morning and knew that I was going to Atlanta that night.

As I taxied out there was a little roughness in the new engine but the mags checked out fine. I took the runway upon the go-ahead from the tower, aimed the nose down the center of the runway, trimmed the rudder and elevators for take-off and moved the throttle forward. As the plane broke ground, I again thought there was a little roughness in the engine but the tachometer responded correctly and I seemed to have the normal amount of takeoff power.

Slightly disconcerted, I climbed straight out to about 1,800 feet, trying to detect anything wrong. Just as I decided to turn to the left to pick up my course for Atlanta, the engine quit! The normal, rational thing to do would have been, along with other cockpit checks, to switch fuel tanks. However, my feeling that I had plenty of fuel must have blocked my normal reactions. Later on the ground I realized that under the stress of wondering what had gone wrong and calling the tower to tell them I was going to make an emergency landing in a direction opposite to my take-off, I didn't go through an adequate check procedure. The tower cleared the runway and asked whether I could glide in from my position. I said something about certainly trying to do so. I congratulated myself on how cool I was and how well I was thinking.

A full five seconds before I hit I could see I was not going to be able to glide as far as the runway. The ground between me and the airport was a plowed field, the furrows at right angles to my flight path. I slowed my speed as much as possible before we finally began to dig into the

The A36A Mustang firing its .50-calibres

furrows, the rad scoop under the wing's center section catching first. Unconsciously, I took off my sunglasses and hung them on the throttle quadrant. Consciously, I put my left hand up on the front of the gun-sight housing to protect my face if I lunged forward during the rapid deceleration. The shoulder straps must've been set just right, for my nose hit the back of my hand with only a slight blow. Then we came to a smooth stop after a very bumpy second or two.

It took me little time to unbuckle the straps and hop out of the cockpit. I scrambled out on the left wing, ran to the end and stepped off the tip which was no more than a foot off the ground. I was naturally apprehensive that something might begin to burn, but there was no sign of any such danger. I noticed some men coming from the adjoining field, for they had seen my strange landing approach with wheels up and short of the runway. I knew I had time to get my sunglasses out of the cockpit before they would arrive, so I walked back to the side of the plane and mounted the wing. I could not find the glasses but I did note that all the fuel gauges read 'full' with the exception of the fuselage tank. I looked at the fuel-selection lever. It was on 'fuselage tank'! I turned the lever to 'left tank' as I dimly remembered some admonition about always taking off on 'left'.

The men who came running were a group of German prisoners and, I dramatised, were all ready to become heroes by pulling me out of a flaming cockpit if need be. One of the guards asked if I was hurt.

I put my hand to my face and said, "Well, I can't feel my nose."

As my hand came down he said, "It looks all right, so it just must be numb."

I happily agreed as we began to take my things out of the cockpit and my luggage out of the rear compartment. An operator in the tower had made some facetious remark about getting the crash crew on its way before I had turned off the radio, but I don't remember when that was. We could hear some sirens wailing as a fire-engine, some cars and a crash truck approached in the distance. Not wanting to get stuck in the plowed field, they stopped at the edge of the nearest road to send out a land party to examine and determine the best route.

Someone helped me carry my things to a staff car which had also arrived nearby and within minutes I was walking into the office of the flight surgeon for the required physical examination. Then I had to report to base operations for a preliminary accident report. By the time all the quizzing was finished and all the papers had been signed, a couple of hours had gone by. On my way back to the squadron operations building, I had to go by the repair shop where I could see a derrick was just lifting the wounded bird off a flat-bed trailer which had hauled it in from the field.

When I got back to the operations room, my sun glasses were hanging on the bulletin board with a note tacked to them, saying, "These were hanging on the throttle quadrant which is why they could not be found on the cockpit floor." We searched the floor twice before I had left the crash scene, thinking that I must've dropped them and that they would have slid forward when the plane stopped.

The next day things happened rapidly. Late in July, my commanding officer and I had put in for early release from the service. Higher powers had decided that things were not going to last long in the Pacific and that those who desired to be released, if they already had a combat tour behind them, might be able to accomplish it. My CO and I had dreams of getting back to college to commence graduate studies so we had made out all the papers required.

VJ Day had come on August 14, while I was putting in an hour in a Mustang. We had a 'stand-down' for 72 hours, as I recall, starting on the 15th. I suppose the top brass didn't want to take any chances with pilots killing themselves by flying while they were celebrating the surrender of the Japanese.

On the 19th I had more paper work to perform concerning the accident. On the 20th I received orders to depart for Fort Devens in Massachusetts for release from active duty. On August 31 at Devens I was processed for release, my terminal leave to expire on the 28th of September when I would revert to inactive status in the Reserve. It was all over, more or less!

I found out a couple of things by mail from my roommate at Stuttgart who was to remain there for a couple of months. First, he said that the crew chief of my ill-fated P-51D had been on leave when the order came through to reduce the fuel load in the fuselage tank to 15 gallons. He had been back just a day prior to the stand-down and had been preflighting the aircraft every day using this same tank. He had probably run it down to practically empty from 15 gallons. If he had done it one more day it might've quit on him right on the ramp! I had assumed he had groomed the plane for the long flight. He had assumed it did not need refueling. Neither of us had checked the total fuel load carefully. At that time I was not aware of Murphy's Law, but I have often thought about it since!

I also wrote to my roommate to send my leather flying jacket which I thought I may have left in the locker at the flight line. But his message was "Tough luck!" When things got hectic with so many people pulling out of the base quickly, some wise guys had gone through the lockers and picked up all articles which they figured would not be missed immediately. He also included a 3rd Air Force Accident Summary and marked one paragraph which referred to my unfortunate experience. Here is the condensed version:

> "P-51 accident, Stuttgart AFB, August 18, 1945. Pilot reported engine detonation before and shortly after take-off. Engine failure at 1,800 feet dictated rapid return to field. Distance was too great. Subsequent forced landing was made in soft plowed field, wheels up. Inspection indicated a trace of metal filings in fuel strainer. No other problems were detected. Pilot no longer available for questioning due to separation from the service."

Mustang Comments

The A-36 was a beautiful aircraft in every way and we had a special affection for it. We felt it was perfect for our work.

We would arrive at the target at 12,000 feet, then drop to 10,000 feet as we approached, to increase our speed and to throw off the tracking of the German ack-ack. We'd open the dive brakes and roll onto our backs as directly above the target as we could estimate, then let the nose fall through until it was lined up on the target. The speed would increase to 375 mph as we descended, giving us a known amount of time to concentrate upon aiming.

We would trip the bombs anywhere from 3,000 to 2,000 feet above the target, but as close to 2,000 feet as we could and sometimes lower. Then we would start the pull-out. Sometimes we would be lower than 1,000 feet when we completed the pull-out and closed the brakes. We would often then dive lower as our speed increased and begin strafing.

Capt. John B. Watson
USAAF
AO-795673

U-Boat Off Norway

Most of my flying was done on convoy duty in Grumman Wildcats, with the Royal Naval Volunteer Reserve. But, my most memorable experience happened when I was on the aircraft carrier HMS *Nabob*.

I joined 852 Squadron aboard the carrier in August, 1944. Nabob was almost entirely Canadian-run and had been commissioned in the spring of that year in the US, where most of these carriers were built. She then came over to the UK and picked up her squadron in July.

On this particular occasion, sometime in the middle of August, we were operating together with the armoured carriers, *Indefatigable*, *Formidable*, *Furious* and the escort carrier *Trumpeter*. We were there to mount a strike against the German battleship *Tirpitz* which was lying in Kaa fjord. It was about 4 o'clock in the afternoon and we were still at action stations, which meant no one was allowed below deck except if you had essential business there. It was a pleasant day, the sun was shining and the sea was calm. There wasn't much happening, so I thought I'd just go below deck and take a shower.

I was right in the middle of my shower when, all of a sudden, there was a loud bang! At first I didn't think too much of the noise because depth charges had been exploding on and off all day as the escort went about their job of ferreting out any lurking U-Boats, but it did sound a little different. Then the alarm bells went off! I got out of the shower and grabbed my trousers. Everything else was in my cabin and I wasn't going to bother going back there. I ran into the companionway and joined other members of the crew making their way to the top deck. Coming to the air crew ready room, I grabbed a fur-lined flying jacket, a Mae West and a pair of flying boots, put them all on and continued on to the flight deck.

What had happened was that an acoustic torpedo had hit the ship at the stern, just beneath the water line. A second torpedo missed us but caught one of our escorting destroyers, which was listing badly and spewing smoke and steam. it took me 5 minutes to get up to the flight deck but by that time the other ships in the fleet were way off on the horizon and there we were with this stricken destroyer, plus another which was desperately trying to protect us and pick up the U-Boat's trail.

We were sitting in the water like that for possibly half an hour. Things didn't seem to get any worse and the ship seemed fairly stable. Meanwhile, the destroyers from the fleet were dropping depth charges in order to get the U-Boat, while aircraft from the other carriers patrolled overhead. Work was also continuing with the rescuing of survivors from the sinking destroyer. It was then announced that the ship was in no danger of sinking but that all air crew, consisting of pilots, navigators, air-gunners and ground staff, would be transferred to one of the destroyers. Even though the sea was calm it was surprising how much those small ships rose and fell, and it was a tricky job to jump from the carrier to the destroyer. They took most of the squadron but a few of us, including myself, were left behind.

Sometime later the decision was made to start up the engines. The Captain, a Canadian named Horatio Nelson Ley who later became a Rear Admiral, announced we were going to make our way back to Scapa Flow, the base for the Home Fleet and about 700 nautical miles away.

The U-Boat was still in the area, having been up on the Asdic. Rather than detach our lone destroyer to look for it, it was decided that two aircraft would be launched and attempt to locate and sink the U-Boat. Now, our ship was riding down by the stern about 15 degrees and

HMS Nabob just minutes after the torpedo hit. — *Royal Navy*

The escorting destroyer which caught the second torpedo. — *Royal Navy*

The HMS Nabob, a sitting duck in the water.　　　　　　— *Royal Navy*

Dumping the aircraft to lighten the load.　　　　　　— *Royal Navy*

we were travelling no more than 7 or 8 knots. If the U-Boat surfaced it could pass us in the dark, with its superior speed, submerge again and lie in wait. Although it was starting to get dark, two crews volunteered to fly the mission and their Avengers were quickly hooked up to the catapult and flown off. They searched for about an hour, but couldn't locate the sub.

Now came the ticklish business of getting these two aircraft back on the carrier. It was night and none of our pilots had landed in the dark. The first Avenger went into the barrier, which was a wire mesh that caught the plane if it missed the arrester wires. The second plane made a perfect landing. We went through the rest of the night without any further harassment from U-Boats.

The following day the damage control team assessed the damage. It was now revealed that the torpedo entered below the mess decks, killing about twenty-five men and creating a very significant bulge in the hangar deck. The bulkheads had to be reinforced because the danger was that if the weather conditions worsened, then the sea would come through the hole and cause sufficient pressure on the bulkheads to burst them. If that happened it was only a matter of time before the ship went down. I remember, too, that in the middle of the bulge in the hangar deck there was a small hole and you could watch the water shooting up, just like a whale's breathing hole. I'm sure the chief engineer was getting pretty fed up being asked how things were. His standard reply was, "As long as the weather holds, we'll hold!"

To lighten the carrier and stay afloat we threw ammunition, several aircraft and any other excess equipment over the side. The last night was the worst because the weather had started to deteriorate. The sea was beating against the bulkhead and we were wondering if the ship would hold up. We were worried, too, that the Germans might make a last determined effort and send out their bombers to sink us for good.

The weather held, however, and it took us just over four days, at an average of 150 miles a day, to get back to Scapa Flow.

Nabob was repaired and later used as a troop carrier, but never used for front line duty

The Wildcat on patrol

again. After the war it was converted to a merchant ship and in this capacity continued to provide useful service for many years.

Wildcat Comments

It was smaller and stubbier than the other Grumman model, the *Hellcat*, but the big difference was that the Wildcat's undercarriage was manually operated. Whenever you took off you had to wind like mad to get that undercarriage up; eighteen turns, according to one pilot who counted. When you left the carrier you didn't really have all that much airspeed and there was a tendency, as you went over the bow, for the aircraft to dip. So, at the same time as you were winding you were watching that you didn't lose airspeed or height, or else you might land in the ocean. I don't know of anyone who did land in the ocean but it was a constant threat. For those watching from the ship there was an almost audible sigh of relief as the aircraft, undercarriage safely home, started to climb.

The Wildcat was an excellent aircraft to fly. It was very maneuverable and very rugged, too. When you would put it down on the deck, particularly in rough weather, you pretty well had to drop it from about 8 feet. If you did the same thing with the Naval version of the Spitfire the Seafire you'd probably collapse the undercarriage.

The Wildcat was ideally suited for operating from escort carriers in the uncertain weather conditions of the North Atlantic. It was also well armed with four machine guns, and with auxiliary tanks had an endurance of well over four hours.

Sub-Lieut (A) George Roberts
RNVR

Strafing an Ammo Dump

On my 70th mission, April 20, 1945, our squadron was vectored to a huge ammunition dump complex near Zethain on the Elve River, north of Riesa, Germany. Previous medium-bomber raids had caused only superficial damage and now we were supposed to do the job using the P-47 Thunderbolt's eight .50-calibre machine guns! Everyone knew that you weren't supposed to strafe ammo dumps!

As we attacked the complex I saw one of our pilots turn away from the target without firing his guns as a stiff 20mm cannon barrage covered the area. Now it was my turn to attack. I went down fast and low, taking evasive action into the target. When I fired my guns at 400 yards there was a tremendous explosion jarring the aircraft circling about a mile and a half above me. Everything I could see was a mass of boiling flames and debris. A hunk of debris shattered my canopy, knocking me unconscious. Luckily, I had turned on 100% oxygen and trimmed my ship so that it was in a gentle nose-high climb when I regained consciousness.

Knowing the ship was badly damaged I got ready to bail out. I unfastened my harness and pulled the emergency canopy ejector handle, but the canopy failed to jettison! I could roll the canopy back electrically, however, and now figured on a belly landing or even the hope of making it back to our home base at Fritzlar, south of Kassel, Germany.

I called on my wingman to take me home as my airspeed indicator and most of the instruments had been knocked out in the explosion. He couldn't; he forgot to bring his maps with him! So, with my maps in my lap and the slipstream tearing through the canopy, I tried to get us both home. In the meantime Captain W.B. Thompson, who had been caught in a subsequent explosion, was trying to get his Thunderbolt to the friendly airfield at Gotha. I could hear on my radio how he finally couldn't control his ship any longer and bailed out; unsuccessfully, with his body landing in downtown Gotha. It was his 105th mission. Our explosions continued into the next day and between us we were supposed to have killed several hundred German troops guarding the complex at Zethain.

Upon landing at Fritzlar I was amazed at my composure and having got nothing worse than a bump on the side of my head. I climbed down from the ship and stood on the ground to fill out the Form 1 using the wing as a support, but I just couldn't hold the pencil.

Thunderbolt Comments

The terms we used for it were 'T-Bolt', 'Bucket of Bolts', and as the models got bigger and heavier with sluggish results, the 'Mush Wagon'.

We loved the ship, especially for fighter-bomber work — the wide landing gear, rugged frame and engine and the eight .50-calibre machine guns. But sometimes, coming out of a dive, or at low-level strafing runs, when you pulled the nose up, the ship had a tendency to keep going down and smash into the ground!

Those few hours in the cockpit, whether in training or combat, were my most exciting moments!

1st/Lt. Sam B. Lutz Jr
USAAF
0-774223

Sam Lutz the day after the raid on the ammunition dump near Zethain.

The Martlesham Playboys

Our aerodrome, Martlesham Heath, was located on the coast about seventy miles northeast of London, in a section of England known as East Anglia.

We were proud men that comprised the 356th Fighter Group. My squadron was the 360th. To me there was none other like it. I know every fighter pilot felt that way about his outfit, but it would be difficult to live with any group of men during such times, fighting together, drinking together, sharing both happiness and sorrow, without feeling that way. Some might call it "Esprit de Corps" but it was something much deeper and closer to the heart.

It was "Axis Sally", who broadcast her propaganda from Berlin several times during the day, that gave our group its name, "The Martlesham Playboys." She obviously didn't hold us in too high regard, as the name might imply. Although she would have everyone believe that we were taking the war rather lightly, she was continually berating us for some dastardly deed such as strafing one of the Luftwaffe's aerodromes before their pilots were out of the sack and ready to receive us. According to Sally we were sneaks and cowards for not sending formal notice of our early arrival. She would then threaten us with annihilation or at least an equally savage attack from one of the Luftwaffe's crack squadrons who, she would say, had been hunting the skies for days trying to engage us in combat, and that we, "The Martlesham Playboys," had been doing our best to elude them. The way she put it you could just picture our entire group hiding behind some big black cloud until the Luftwaffe gave up their search in disgust and flew back home.

We hardly ever missed one of Sally's broadcasts if we could help it. Aside from her hopeless attempts at hair-raising propaganda, which was always a barrelful of laughs, the entire program was nicely interspaced with a fine selection of classical and semi-classical music; much better than the BBC had to offer. The funny part of it all was that Sally thought she was really getting under our skins, whereas actually it had quite the reverse effect on us.

Our Group flew Thunderbolts. We most affectionately called them 'Jugs'. Weighing seven and one-half tons, heavy for a fighter, they still had power to spare with their Pratt & Whitney R-2800 engine and the new paddle-blade prop. We usually carried two 500-pound bombs in addition to our six or eight .50-calibre machine guns which were capable of literally tearing a target apart. Some of us had two machine guns removed, one from each wing, which meant we could carry more ammunition and fire longer.

The Thunderbolt in action

We all knew the Thunderbolt would never let us down, that we could subject it to the worst rigors of aerial combat and it would hold together and bring us home. The Thunderbolt was the first aircraft able to fly fast enough to run into the sound barrier which could rip an aircraft to pieces.

I recall one day rolling my 'Jug' over on its back at about 28,000 feet and letting it fall through. In seconds I was plummeting straight down. The engine screamed and my speed built up rapidly. In nothing flat I was in compressibility. The controls became rigid. I braced my feet and with all my strength I still couldn't move the stick. For probably 10,000 feet or more I plummeted earthward. Somewhere around 15,000 feet my controls once again began to respond as I reached the denser air. I made my pull-out as gradual as I could but the G-forces were tremendous and the gray-out inevitable. When the gray shade lifted, the old 'Jug' was back at 10,000 feet going straight up. This proved several things to me. First was that I was a horse's neck for getting myself into a situation like that, second I was very fortunate to have gotten out of it and, last I knew the Thunderbolt was indestructible. I was so embarrassed about the whole thing, I didn't breath a word of what happened back at the aerodrome.

Capt. H. Phillip Causer
USAAF
AO799937

The First Sortie

At No. 59 OTU in England I met a fellow named Colin Fallon, an Australian. He had joined the RAAF in 1940 and later came to the UK where he did some drogue towing while awaiting an OTU course. The drogue towing was on Lysanders and it was during this period that he suffered his first accident, turning an aircraft upside down after blowing a tire on landing. He suffered a serious back injury and endured several months of hospitalization before finally reaching No. 59 OTU and joining my course.

We quickly became good friends and he impressed me with his dedication and determination to become a useful squadron member, and hopefully enter a theatre of war that involved the Japanese. The Japanese forces at that time were threatening Darwin in northern Australia, and Colin felt for this situation very keenly.

We graduated from OTU and were posted to the South-East Asia Command, leaving the UK on December 18, 1942 and sixty-four days later arriving in Bombay, India. Following yet another refresher course at Rawalpindi, India, the great day finally arrived and we were posted to 261 Squadron RAF, then stationed at Chittagong, where we were to fly Hurricane IIB's.

Colin was very happy to be posted to a squadron in the Japanese theatre and was most impatient to carry out his first operational sortie. He waited a long time for this moment. After enlisting in 1940 and after three long years of training, accidents, and hospitalization, he had finally made it.

On June 27, 1943, our squadron was assigned to escort a squadron of Vultee Vengeance dive-bombers to bomb the Japanese-held airfield on Akyab Island, off the Arakan coast in the Bay of Bengal. Colin and myself were to fly in a section of four, led by Australian Flying Officer Norman Rankin. Colin was in the midst of writing a letter to his wife, a nurse in New South Wales, when word came through for 261 to get airborne and rendezvous with the Vengeance squadron over Chittagong. As we ran to our aircraft, Colin gave me a slap on the back, saying, "Well, Woodie, we finally made it, after all these years."

The flight to Akyab was uneventful and we encountered some light flak over the airfield. After the Vengeance squadron had finished their bombing we turned for home, and it was then that I noticed smoke coming from Colin's aircraft. He entered into a shallow dive and headed out into the Bay of Bengal. Norm Rankin and myself followed him, trying to get him on the intercom but with little success. We entered a low layer of cloud and as we emerged, Colin was in a spin and still smoking. We still circled his aircraft, attempting to contact him. We could see him struggling to recover from the spin, which he finally did, only to over-correct on pullout and stall again. This time he was too low to recover and after three or four turns he crashed into the Bay! Rankin and I circled the spot. The Hurricane broke up and sank very quickly, leaving only an oil patch and a few bits of wreckage.

As we headed back to Chittagong, I could not believe that it had all ended so quickly for Colin. After all those years of training and yearning for action, it was all over in one hour and 20 minutes and he had not even fired one shot in anger.

When I got back to the base, the half-completed letter to his wife awaited me, which I forwarded on to her, with a short note telling her what had transpired. Then the adjutant made the official notification, and that was it.

Hurricane comments

When I first flew it in 1943 it was considered too slow and certainly lacked the maneuverability of a Spitfire or a Mustang. The Hurricane was a very pleasant aircraft to fly and was light on the controls, but was no match for the land-based version of the Japanese Zero. As a result we were cautioned not to stay around and dog fight, but rather to dive and zoom if possible, and get in and get out fast.

The Hurricane had no particular vices and carried considerable firepower. The IIB had eight .303's and the IIC had four 20mm cannons, with the cannons on the IIC making a dramatic fall off in airspeed after a 3-second burst.

Most pilots who flew the Hurricane were very loyal to it, even though it was often outclassed in aerial combat. However, we used it on Army support work and strafing airfields and enemy troop locations right up to the end of the war in Burma.

One feature we found frustrating when learning to fly the Hurricane was the location of the undercarriage traction lever. It was forward and down low, on the right-hand side. After take-off it was necessary to change hands on the control column and lean forward to retract the undercarriage with the right hand. As a result, when first learning, the tendency was to push the control column slightly forward when leaning over. It provided for some hair-raising take-offs, particularly if you had a short reach.

F/O Frank Woodrow
RCAF
J87077

Hawker Hurricane IIC with four 20mm cannons

B-24 Liberator under flak

'The Italian-North African Campaign'
—the bombers and fighters who operated out of the south

What's a Hole in a B-24!

I enlisted in the Army Air Forces at Fort Snelling, in St. Paul, Minnesota. We were inducted and while waiting for a posting we were required to do general duties such as cleaning up the grounds, shovelling snow & KP duty. The sergeant in charge of the mess hall requested that I stay with their area on the KP, but being young and wanting to fly, I simply said, "No thanks."

From St. Paul I was sent down to Amarillo, Texas for my basic training. It was like every basic training; rough, tough, long, hard days and nights but with all these new experiences and learning, time flew by and it all seemed like fun.

While we were here we were segregated out as to what facet of the Air Force we were going to belong to. We took some aptitude tests, then were taken to a big hall. There must have been a thousand men in there. The officer in charge stood up on the centre stage and shouted out, "OK, how many of you gentlemen want to be pilots?"

Almost 99.9 percent of the hands went up. "Well," he said, "We've got to have some other men on the airplane. We can't all be pilots. So, how many want to be navigators?" A few hands went up. Then he shouts, "How many bombardiers?" A few guys raised their hands. So on and so forth down the line. The he said, "Now here's the question I always ask but never get any response. How many of you want to be gunners in the Air Force?" And two people put up their hands; my buddy and I! So then the officer said, "Boy, it looks like we got a couple of crazy ones in the crowd;" but that didn't bother me because I was always interested in hunting and guns ever since I was a kid.

Anyway, we finished off our basic training, then my buddy and I were sent down to the Bombing and Gunnery School at Harlingen, Texas.

When we got to Harlingen you want to know who else showed up there? The other 1,000 guys who were in our class! We were all sent there to be gunners! Back in Amarillo the officers knew all along we were going to end up there.

I liked the gunnery training. We used .45 automatics, submachine guns, .30-calibre carbines, shotguns and .50-calibres on a gun range.

For one part of it they put you on the back of a pick-up truck which had a flat bed on it. Then they drive you onto an oval race track. On the perimeter of the track were houses where clay pigeons were shot out and they would go in all directions. You'd start by going about 5 miles-per-hour, then faster each time around. On the flat bed was a Browning automatic shotgun mounted into a Bell adapter. Your partner fed shells into the gun for you. You also had to spend your time in the trap houses and being near the most southernly part of the U.S. it was hot inside the house, just like a sauna. I did quite well at the shooting because I got the highest mark ever achieved on that range.

My next stop was Lincoln, Nebraska. It was here that we were put into our bomber crews, then sent to Pueblo, Colorado for advanced training on B-24 Liberators, where I was a tail-gunner.

Before going overseas we were sent to Topeka, Kansas, where we were actually given the plane that we would fly to the combat zone; a B-24L series.

We flew from Topeka to Bangor, Maine and then Goose Bay, Labrador, before crossing part of the ocean and landing at Iceland. After a week at Iceland we flew off and landed at Valley, Wales, where we shared an airfield with the RAF.

After about a week we left there and landed at French Morocco. We spent a few days there before going on to Bari, Italy. We were there another few days before getting stationed at Cerignola, just south of Foggia, with the 458th Bomber Group, 459th Bomber Squadron.

My whole combat record consisted of six missions. On them we went to northern Italy and north and south Austria. We hit marshalling yards and provided bomber support for the Army when they were moving through the Po Valley.

I'll never forget my last mission.

We went on a run to Austria that day and ran into a real pile of flak. You've probably heard the expression that "the flak was so heavy you could walk on it". Well that day was just like that.

We were flying along through the flak when I heard a bang, then a series of small bangs. A piece of flak had come into the plane, rolled around for a while and because we were flying forward, had worked its way to the back of the plane. It then hit me in the back of my flying jacket and fell to the floor. I still have that piece of flak. It was a small piece of 88mm.

Then one big piece of flak hit on the leading edge of one wing; but we weren't too worried. Heck, it was only a hole. What's a hole in a B-24!

After the mission we were coming back and the pilot said to the co-pilot, "OK, put the landing gear down."

The co-pilot pulled the lever; the wheels started down but then they stopped part way down! As it was doing this we could see all the hydraulic fluid going out of the hole in the wing. The flak had hit the hydraulic system and all the fluid was lost.

You've probably heard stories about crews urinating in the hydraulic system to try and get the wheels down. Well, we poured everything into it. After a short while we finally got the wheels down, but the wheels still hadn't locked into position. This meant that the wheels might collapse when we touched down. The pilot wasn't too worried, because he said we could manually drop the nose wheel, then hook up a couple of parachutes to the ball turret and throw them out the waist windows to act as brakes to stop the plane.

We hooked the chutes up, but it wasn't easy. It took two guys holding and two guys pulling to pull the rip cords.

Then the pilot said, "Everybody else go to the tail." So, everybody went to the back, except my buddy and myself as we were going to throw the chutes out on both sides of the aircraft.

So, we're coming to our base and we're set up to land on a special dirt landing strip that was used only for crash-landings. We were coming in low and the pilot gently set the wheels down, and the wheels didn't collapse! The pilot screamed out, "I think we made it. The wheels are holding! They're holding! I'm going to ease the nose wheel down now."

Well, he eased the nose down and as soon as the wheels hit the ground it collapsed! The other two wheels didn't collapse but the darn nose wheel, the one that was supposed to be working, didn't hold up. We went from 100 miles-per-hour to zero in about 50 feet. The Lib went nose-first into the ground, and everybody in the tail wasn't in the tail anymore. They were on top of my buddy and myself, and all of us ended up in the bomb-bay rear bulkard.

After it was all over, we looked around at each other and nobody was hurt. Not a scratch on any of us! No fires either because the pilot cut the switches on impact.

After getting out of the plane one of the crew, having removed the clip from his .45, was clearing his gun. This was standard procedure. When he did that he sliced his hand with the slide! That was the only thing that happened.

Whenever a crew crash-lands, they ground you for 30 days. We took this of course, and then on the 31st day when we were scheduled to fly, the war ended.

Liberator Comments

The Lib flew like a big bird; the wings would actually flap. As long as the wings were flapping you had nothing to worry about.

I really liked it. It was a good, functional aircraft but when you compare it to the B-17 Flying Fortress, it was like comparing a Cadillac to a Model T. The Fortress had more crew comforts. Each crew position had its own comfortable area, not like the B-24. The Lib had a bigger bombload, though.

We used to call the B-24 the 'Whistling S--thouse' because the wind used to whistle through it like crazy. The wind was so strong, you could hardly light a cigarette in the plane.

S/Sgt. Richard Wirth
USAAF
37591726

'Axis Sally' was Right

Each evening after supper, the one thing we always did was check the bulletin board to see if we were scheduled for a mission the next day. After that I made it a point to walk over to the tent of the enlisted men in my crew. I checked on their well-being, the general state of their health and made certain there was no reason they would not be fit enough to fly the next day. I also told them about the gas load. A full load of gasoline meant a long mission. This time the bulletin board indicated a full load.

The date was October 2, 1944. The place; Pantanella, Italy. I was with 782 Bomb Squadron, 465 Bomb Group, 55 Wing, 15th Air Force.

Our new Officer's Club was nearly completed and the poker game was in progress. I sat in on the game with about seven others. From the very beginning luck was not with me, so after losing about 30 dollars I left the game. I watched for a while and saw Captain Farber, another pilot, drop considerably more money. It had been my observation that when your luck ran bad in one thing, it ran bad in others, too.

At about 03:30 on October 3, 1944, we got the wake up call. I roused co-pilot Al Frick, our navigator Pete Redder, and Cliff Boyce, our bombardier, and headed for the mess hall and then to the briefing room.

The powdered eggs were great. The so-called bacon was greasy. Just the right thing to start us off on what could be the last day of our lives.

Fully sated, we headed for the converted stable that served as our briefing room. Arriving late, as always, most of the seats were taken and Frick and I stood at the rear of the room.

Having picked up my 'Flak Flimsy' off the table, I saw our position near the rear of the formation. That was nothing new. I had been there on many previous trips. The target was new, though: the Manzel Aircraft Works, Friedrichshafen, Germany. They were the makers of ball bearings for the Luftwaffe; a real prime target. One we would like to put out of existence.

The briefing droned on. The weather men promised clear skies, and the intelligence men stated how little flak we would be encountering and how little fighter activity. The 'ground grippers' nearly put us to sleep telling us what a snap this mission was going to be, but from past missions we had learned they were not always correct about their predictions. Every time, they sweated out our return to find out how accurate they had been.

We then 'hacked' our watches so that we would all start our engines at the same time, all taxi at the same time, rendezvous at the same time, hit the IP (Initial Point) together and arrive in a bunch over the target. 'Hacking' was a waste of time, but at least we all had the same time on our watches.

We started the engines and then played follow the leader, right to the target and back to base.

We taxied to the parallel runways and made our take-offs, alternating at 30 second intervals. We taxied with our flaps up so as not to have stones blown up into the flap area and jam their movement.

In our turn we dropped flaps and roared down the runway. A couple of pilots were known to have not put down their flaps and without the extra lift used up the whole 5,000-foot runway and flew through the area of the British gun crew, placed foolishly between and just beyond the west end of the parallel runways.

I made my usual take-off run. I held the Lib on the ground, beyond its normal take-off speed and then pulled the aircraft into a steep climb, over the prop-wash of the preceding plane without the usual wrestling of the controls. This was not the standard procedure, but was something I learned after nearly being killed on my second mission.

To-day's mission looked like a success. We hit the target, or close to it, and were heading home. There was a little banter on the intercom about the mission being a milk run. I didn't like that kind of talk. After all, we were not yet to the Alps. We had a long way to go and the thought went through my mind about hearing 'Axis Sally' on the radio remark about how the Officer's Club of the 782nd Bomb Squadron was nearing completion, and about the tight formation we were flying. She went on to say that one day soon we could expect a visit from the Luftwaffe.

At about this time the leader of our seven plane box was having a little engine trouble. Also Captain Farber, flying just opposite me, wanted to change places. His co-pilot was having trouble flying cross-cockpit and it would be easier for him to fly on a wing.

By the time the change was completed the leader of our box had feathered one engine and the rest of the twenty-odd other planes of our group were about 5 miles ahead of us, leaving us out there like sitting ducks. Repeated calls by the leader of our box to the flight group leader were of no avail. He wasn't going to slow down for anybody.

Then, over the intercom came two chilling sentences. "Here they come! Six of them!" We all knew who 'them' were.

The twin 'fifties' of my engineer, Bob Haught, in the top turret barked and filled the cockpit with dust and the floor with spent casings. Co-pilot Frick was doing the flying at the time and looking out the window I saw an Me-109 just edging up and over my left wing. It was so close I could see the dead pilot with his head down, starting his spiraling dive to earth! He missed my plane at the last instant and Haught got credit for a kill.

At the same time the fighters on the right headed for the group in front, the ones that should have waited for us but didn't. Of the three fighters on the left, one was killed and one hit Captain Farber's plane. In a matter of seconds our seven plane box was down to two.

Not wanting to wait around for a second attack I decided to rejoin the rest of the group. I took over the controls and at the same time pushed my seat back. Frick must've thought I was going to bail out and he was going to beat me to the bomb-bay. I pushed him back into his seat. I then ran the propellers up to 2,700 RPM and advanced the Honeywell superchargers to Number 10. With the resulting noise, Haught dropped down from his guns thinking we had runaway props. I indicated that I had applied full power.

We left the one remaining plane from the seven plane box and headed for the safety of the other group some 5 miles in front.

I had that old B-24 doing 225 indicated at about 30,000 feet which was quite a feat. Off to the left and another 2,000 feet or so higher was Farber's plane with a raging fire aboard and no one in our crew reporting seeing any chutes.

Coming up on the rest of the group I was doing about 50 miles an hour more than the cruising speed of 170. My next problem was getting my plane to slow down so that I didn't fly right past the group. So, I chopped the power and I still came on. I wondered if the flaps would stay on if they were dropped. I though about dropping the gear for extra drag but I didn't know if the fighters were still in the area. Remembering that lowering the gear is a signal of surrender, I thought better of that.

We slowed down just as we approached the group and I nosed my plane right up and under the tail of the last plane. The tail-gunner had his twin fifties pointed right at me. He was about 10 feet away. He wasn't taking any chance that we might be Germans flying a captured Lib. In a little bit I eased away and got into formation with the rest of the group.

Coming down to an altitude where we could take off our oxygen masks, I always went to the back of the plane to talk to the crew to assess any possible damage we might have sustained. My inspection revealed three apparent bullet holes in the right wing in the area of the wheel well.

On arriving at the field I notified the tower that I would be landing last, figuring that with a flat tire I might tear up the metal landing strip if the gear collapsed.

I made the landing holding the right wheel off as long as I could. There was no flat.

Arriving back at the hardstand I was greeted by Mel Mihalski, an armourer, who belonged to the same Cheektowaga (New York) Alcoves baseball team with me back home. He made another one who was happy with our safe return.

That night in the officers' mess we were twenty men short. Five planes failed to return. 'Axis Sally' was right.

Liberator Comments

The Liberator did not get the publicity of the B-17 Flying Fortress but, to my mind, the Lib was a superior aircraft. I think Boeing Aircraft Corporation must have employed a full division in publicity alone. Any time a Fort did anything it appeared in the news. It was annoying to us *Lib* drivers.

Both planes carried about the same bomb load, flew about the same distance and went to the same altitude, but the B-24 cruised at an indicated 175 miles-per-hour while the B-17 did only 150. You can forget all about that 300 MPH jazz. Let me tell you, that 25 miles an hour made quite a difference. On a 4-hour trip to a target, the same target as us, we would get there half an hour sooner and get home about an hour quicker.

The B-24 Liberator was heavy on the controls. Two months after I stopped flying them I still had calluses on my left hand. It was the fastest at that time, but slow by today's standards.

Liberators didn't glide worth a damn. Any real engine problems and you looked beneath you for a spot to land. That was due to the wing being a modified Davis airfoil but it was that same wing that made for the speed at which it could cruise.

The Lib was a stable aircraft. It bounced very little in the air. On the way down there was a little rocking due to prop-wash, but nothing to mention. And once you got the mains down, you were down. Rarely did the Lib bounce or float. It was a pleasure to land.

In conclusion, I know the B-24 Liberator was the best heavy bomber in the United States Army Air Forces.

F/O William Bruce Jr.
USAAF
T-61594

Back Row L to R: Cliff Boyce bombardier; Peter Reder, navigator; Al Frick, co-pilot; Bill Bruce, pilot. Mid Row: Chuck Cannon, nose-gunner; Bob Haught, engineer; Aurielius Heath, ball-turret gunner; Elmer Evard, radio-operator. Front Row: Tony D'Alessandro, asst. engineer and Walter Detmering, tailgunner.

PILOTS' FLIMSY   6 August 1944

C. O.	Colonel BULLOCK	Briefing	0430
		Transportation	0515
DEPUTY C. O.	Captain PERRY	Stations	0545
		Start Engines	0610 1st A. U.
2ND DEPUTY			0615 2nd A. U.
		Taxi	0625
2ND ATTACK UNIT	Major ANDRUS	Take-off	0640
		Assembly	0800
DEPUTY	Captain BLACKBURN	Line Rendezvous	0806 11000 feet
2ND DEPUTY		Wing Rendezvous	0819 11000 feet

1. FLIGHT INFORMATION: Gas - 2700
    a. Assembly — 11000 feet - 0800   Ammo.- 4200
    b. Line Rend: CORATO - with 464th - 0806
    c. Wing Rend: SPINAZZOLA - 11000 feet - 0819
    d. Order of Flight & Altitudes:
            460th - 20,000 -- 485th - 21000 -- 465th - 21000 — 464th - 22000
    e. Key Point -- REVELLATA POINT (LAST POINT TO CLIMB) - 11000
    f. I.P. — L'ISLE-SUR-LA-SORGUE
    g. Axis of Attack — 277°   LEAD GROUP FIRES
    h. Target Time — 1200   RR FLARE AT RP
    i. Altitude — 21000   R   FOR CLIMB
    j. Rally -- LEFT 202° to 43 52N - 04 33E
    k. E. T. R. — 1444

2. NAVIGATION INFORMATION

		ALTITUDE	DISTANCE	MAG-HEAD	TIME
CORATO TO ANDRIA		11000			0806
SPINAZZOLA		11000	20	278	0819D
MELFI			110	283	0827
TERRACINA			216	295	0910
REVELLATA POINT	42 35N-08 41E				
(LAST POINT TO START CLIMB)		11000	99	302	1034
43 20N - 06 42E			50	313	1112
MANOSQUE	43 50N-05 47E		32	287	1129
LISLE SUR-LA-SORGUE	43 55N-05 03E(IP)	21000	12	277	1141
AVIGNON RR BRIDGE	(TARGET)	21000	06	209 (1145)	120
43 52N - 04 33E			45	209	11
43 10N - 04 20E			191	111	120
PALAZZO POINT	42 22N-08 33E		221	111	125
TERRACINA			120	98	1405
BASE					1444

3. BOMBING INFORMATION
    a. Target - AVIGNON/RHONE RR BRIDGE
    b. Alternates - WEST HALF MIRAMAS M/Y; - LAST RESORT - VAR RIVER BRIDGE
    c. Bomb load - 10 - 500# RDX - fuse - .1 nose - non delay tail
    d. Window - 2 cartons - dispense 4 units every 20 sec from 2 minutes before
                    I. P. until clear of flak.

Both sides of an official pilot's "Flak Flimsy" report, dated 6 August 1944.
— Bill Bruce (US Army Air Forces photo)

GROUP FORMATION:

SPARE SHIPS:
    Blue "D"
Yellow "D"

"A" BOX

BULLOCK
Blue "I"

HALBACH   PERRY
White "C"   Yellow "P"

KENNEDY
Yellow "B"

GOODWIN   BRUCE
White "E"   White "W"

"C"   WARNACK-SCANLON   "B"
                                              White "S"
        ROBERTS
        Yellow "A"
HURD   SMITH   O'LEARY   PENDLETO
Yellow "M"   Yellow "I"   Blue "P"   Yellow
        ASHLEY   BATES
        Yellow "R"   Blue "B"
BRANCH   WHEELER   BONIN   DUNCAN
Yellow "N"   Yellow "O"   Red "O"   Red "N"
        SCHUSTER   DOYLE
        Yellow "G"   Yellow "C"

2ND ATTACK UNIT
                    "D"
        ANDRUS - PETRANEK
        Red "M"
BROWN   BLACKBURN
Blue "Z"   Red "B"
        JONES
        Blue "C"
OWENS   KARA
Blue "X"   Blue "K"
        JOHNSON
        Blue "B"
                                    "E"
                        TEAGARDEN - FALLENTI
                           Red "C"
                    MOORE   HEFFERNAN
                    Red "D"   Red "S"
                        LESCALLETTE
                        Red "K"
                    HANSELMAN   MORRISON
                    Red "L"   Red "H"
                        VAN SLYKE
                        Yellow "K"

Note Bill Bruce's plan under Box "A" on the Group Formation Page.

Flak over Germany. — *Bill Bruce (US Army Air Forces photo)*

Bomb Group photo showing bombs hitting marshalling yards in Yugoslavia.
— *Bill Bruce (US Army Air Forces photo)*

The Garibaldi Brigade

When I joined the RCAF I wanted to be a Spitfire pilot. That's all I thought about. But of course I was patriotic, too. We all were. I was only 20 years old when I flew ops with a Spitfire squadron. I guess the fighter squadrons wanted their pilots to be young and daring, and maybe a bit reckless; but we had to be disciplined, too.

When you're young you do some crazy things. I can still remember OTU in Egypt. I had just come off Harvards and had taken some flights on Spitfires, but without having to use any oxygen. One day I was supposed to take the Spitfire up to 18,000 feet twice and 25,000 feet once, in that order and with oxygen. The first time I took her up I didn't want to stop at 18,000 because she was still climbing. What a thrill! I eventually got it up to 30,000 feet and played up there for awhile before I came down.

The next time I took the Spitfire up to 32,000 feet, and then I put her into a dive. When I did that the controls froze on me. What a scary feeling that was! I couldn't do a thing until I got down to 3,000 feet, where the controls became free, and from there I could finally level out. Levelling that close to the ground was like riding a buckboard on a gravel road.

When I got to the ground, the chief instructor sure gave me an earful. Then he showed me some classified information. He showed me that a plane can break the sound barrier by going 625 miles-per-hour at 20,000 feet, and said that I was doing close to 625. So, I promised him I'd never take it into another dive. But the next time I went up I took her up to 42,000 feet, just to see what the Spitfire could do.

Our fighter squadron, 417 (City of Windsor Squadron), was exceptional because it was the only Canadian fighter squadron operating outside of England. We were in the Italian Campaign, providing fighter cover for the Canadian 1st and 5th Army and the British Army.

I joined the squadron near Naples in 1944. We lived out of tents and huts, never seeing a building; at least not one we stayed in. Our runways were mostly dirt strips and were sometimes right in the middle of an orchard. When we'd taxi out we could see an occasional Italian run across the road right in front of us. But if one of those guys ever got too close then that was too bad for them because we couldn't stop or steer to one side.

On the afternoon of August 10, 1944, myself and three other pilots went on a weather reconnaisance mission. We left Perugia Aerodrome, an old Italian pre-war airfield, and headed north. Two pilots were to go up the east coast of Italy, while myself and my wing man were to fly up the west coast.

We were about 100 miles behind the lines and well north of Florence, flying at 22,000 feet, when my Spitfire VIII got an air lock. An air lock in the belly tank of a Spit VIII was serious because that meant the motor would quit. I tried everything to get the plane going again, but nothing worked.

I called our base. "This is Rally Red One. My motor quit."

Then I told my wing man, "Rally Red Two, head for base.", but he wanted to go with me. I insisted he go back to base; and he left.

So, I was gradually going down and down. I took until something like 11,000 feet before I could see anything because of very solid cloud cover. Meanwhile, I was still talking to our base. An English fellow who I was in communication with, said, "Give me a 30-second ol' chap, so I can get a fix on you."

And I answered back, "One, two, three, four, five; five, four, three, two, one."

Then he said, rather calmly, too, "Thank you and by the way ol' chap, best of luck." I was on my own.

I jumped out once I hit 6,000 feet but waited till about 4,000 feet before I pulled the cord, so my chute wouldn't be spotted so quickly. When I pulled the cord the chute came open, I remember it was like getting kicked in the ass by a mule.

I was coming down in a straight fall, over a heavily-wooded area with no roads or fields. I could see the Spitfire going off into the distance, hitting a hill, and exploding. About a mile away I saw someone along a path, he looked like an ant, from where I was, and he was shooting at me! I hit the ground right by the edge of a deep, sloping hill, packed up my chute and hid it in some bushes. I saw a tree nearby that had branches touching the ground while the roots were coming out of the ground. So that's where I hid; under the roots. It made great shelter.

That same day, I was still under the tree, I heard people walking around in the bushes. I didn't know who they were and I wasn't curious to find out.

The next day, just before sunset, I got out and walked down a pathway until I came to a barn and a house. I knew two important Italian words, important to me anyway, and they were 'No Tedesco' which meant 'No German'; and 'Inglese' which meant 'English'. I used both words on the farmer and was quite fortunate that most Italians were very sympathetic to the Allied cause.

After speaking these words, the farmer took me into the house and gave me some bread, cheese, and wine. After I had finished eating he showed me to the barn and the straw, and closed the door. Sometime during the night I heard voices, and not wanting to take a chance, burrowed myself deep into the straw. Then they all came into the barn and starting poking around the straw and shining their lanterns, to try and find me. I was scared stiff! I thought for sure I'd be a goner. Then they found me and lifted the straw away. My heart was thumping! I looked up and saw two rifle barrels staring me in the face. They gave me a smoke, then thanked the farmer. I soon found out they were civilians, thank God! Italian partisans. They were on my side!

We walked the rest of the night, over hills and through creeks, until we came to a wooded area and hid there during the day.

That night we walked some more until we approached a few buildings; a church, a priest's home, and five other houses. There weren't any roads around, just mule trails. It was there we met a British Major and a Captain who were both dropped behind the lines to help the partisan movement; and two army privates who escaped from a POW camp and were having such a great time with the partisans that they didn't ever want to go back to their unit. The Major had a short-wave radio and used it, through coded messages, to tell the British forces that Flying Officer Locke was with them and in one piece.

Sometime after this, a mountie and an RCAF officer came to my mother's house in Sydney, Nova Scotia. When she answered the door she had to identify herself as Mrs. Locke, and she needed proof to show who she was. Then she signed a government letter, and they told her that they had word concerning their son. She opened a letter that read, "...your son is not a POW but is behind enemy lines with Allied friends. After reading this letter would you kindly destroy it, as it may jeopardize your son's safety." Up to this point, my mother had only received word that I was missing in action. Anyway, she didn't destroy the letter. She kept it.

For the next three months I stayed with the partisans. In fact I was part of them; the Garibaldi Brigade, as they were called. They gave me an ammunition belt to sling over my shoulder, a couple of grenades and a rifle. We would do things like setting ambushes for German and Italian vehicles and their officers. Then we'd shoot the cars up. Harassment it was called. Anything to bother the enemy.

Spitfire Comments

The most beautiful aircraft ever built. No faults. A pilot could do anything to it and it would get you out of trouble, instead of the other way around like many other planes. Whenever Jerry came out with a better fighter, the British just came out with a better Spitfire.

The Spitfire never quite had the range, it would burn about 50 gallons of gas an hour while cruising and about 120 flat out, because it wasn't built as long-range aircraft. That was its only trouble. But, Oh, it climbed like a homesick angel!

F/O Roland Locke
RCAF
J25483

F/O Roland Locke

Camouflaged Spitfire over the English countryside

J for Johnnie

I flew out of Libya in the Italian-North African Campaign with 178 and 462 Squadrons of the RAF. I was a flight-engineer on the Halifax and I flew twenty-eight missions.

A flight-engineer had a big job to perform. We had to watch, as well as control, the gas consumption and use it to our best advantage. As the big 4-engined bombers came into the war, the Air Force was forced to use flight-engineers as part of a bomber crew. On the Halifax I stayed just under the astrodome, behind the pilot. From there I could see my fuel gauges and I made my calculations. I also had to watch for enemy fighters and give star shots to our navigator for Dead Reckoning Navigation. We weren't on Gee like many other planes were. On Gee there were two stations in England that gave out a signal and you'd just go for the point where they intersected. Not us, we went by the stars.

Flight-engineers had to have at least their Grade Grouping as mechanics before acceptance for Engineers Training; as well as Grade 12 and also some physical conditioning. We also took studies in Morse Code, hydraulics, cooling systems, electronics and gunnery. I had to sub as a mid-upper gunner when under attack by enemy fighters, and I was second dickey on take-offs; namely the co-pilot. If the engines ever caught fire I had to be ready to feather the props.

Did you know that it took about 350 gallons just for the Halifax to get off the ground, then 150 gallons per hour at cruising speed? We had twelve tanks in total, all in the wings, holding 1800 gallons in all. We'd take off on the four main tanks and land on the same four. And did you know that for every 100 gallons less, you could carry 500 more pounds of bombs? As you can see we went on ops with a minimum amount of gas and the maximum of bombs, yet I had to make sure we got the bomber back with some gas to spare. Some engineers would use less gas than others; as much as 400 gallons a trip. We had to take into consideration lots of things such as distance, wind speed, revs, aircraft speed and bomb-load.

Probably our greatest mission on our Mark III Halifax, *J for Johnnie* was the trip to Psyttalei Island just north of Crete. This island was used for defense purposes only. It was heavily defended with many anti-aircraft guns of the 88mm type. The purpose of our mission was to wipe out the island for good!

We went there in four waves. Halifaxes, Liberators and Mitchells were some of the planes and they carried high explosives, fire-bombs and Pathfinder markers which were known as Illuminating Aircraft in the Italian Campaign.

Once we got over the target we were coned by about twenty-five searchlights, besides being attacked by a Ju-88 which we evaded. It was a 7-hour, 10-minute trip, according to my log. When we left the island it was a raging fire!
When a photo-reconnaissance Mosquito flew over the next day, nothing was left!

Halifax Comments

I actually think that the Lancaster was a bit overrated because the Halifax was a good plane, too. Thousands of Halifaxes were built. They had to be good! They could take the punishment required of a big bomber, but back in Canada the Lancaster seemed to get most of the publicity.

F/O Ralph Cook
RCAF
C94238

Bailing Out

Our squadron the 417, was in Italy in 1944 where we provided the fighter cover for the Canadian Army. This particular day we were on an armed recce mission. That meant we had no designated target to shoot at, so we'd try to smash a road, bridge, or railroad. Our strategy was to dive-bomb with our Spitfires, drop the bomb that was tied to our fuselage, then go after another target and strafe it. The Spitfire was never designed for dive-bombing, by the way, but that's another matter.

We were about 150 miles south east of Florence and heard that General Kesserling of the German Army, the top man after the Rommel suicide, was somewhere in our area. We had to watch out for him and his well-armed column, made up of probably the best tanks used during the entire war; the Tiger.

Now let me tell you about the deadly Tiger tank. They were like a mobile anti-aircraft gun. Anybody that flew in North Africa or Italy knows all about them since most of our casualties were from the Tiger. They could fight on the ground with the Army and could also shoot at us fighters when we were in the air. It's a shame the Allies never had anything like it.

On daylight fighter raids we often saw the black puffs from their 88mm shells. When you heard the noise and saw the black puff, then you knew the shells were getting closer. But you still had to keep going. If you saw the puff, heard the noise and smelt the cordite; then you knew they were getting really close! But if you could see the flame even in daylight, then you were hit and it was game over!

One day we spotted a column on a road. We dive-bombed them, then started climbing. I was around 2,000 feet when I heard a loud BAM! I saw the flame and smelled the cordite! I called my No. 2 man because he was young and new to the squadron, and was probably more scared than I was. I said, "No. 2, you OK?"

"Fine," he said back. "That was pretty close!"

"That just took the skin off my teeth!" But as soon as I blurted out the last word, the motor caught fire.

I knew I was close to my own lines and thought I'd just coast the rest of the way. I was gliding toward the lines, with the flames getting hot when I knew I'd have to get out; which was somewhat of a problem in the tight-fitting Spitfire. After some struggling I managed to dive out the door; but to my horror, my chute got caught. I was lower than 1,000 feet by this time and had to get out soon. I pulled myself away and was finally free. A few seconds later I pulled the cord.

I could see I was drifing in the wind and thought I was behind our lines. On the ground I could see people looking up and watching me. It was about 12 noon.

I hit the ground and the wind was pulling me. An Italian fellow was running along side of me with a jug of wine in his hand. I was screaming at the crowd of people to take the air out of the chute because I was bouncing around like a golf ball. All they had to do was collapse the chute, then I could stand up. But they wouldn't help me out. Meanwhile, the women in the group were feeling the silk of the chute like they were at a Sears bargain sale.

Finally some Canadian soldiers came and collapsed the chute for me and I stood up and took it off. Then the Italian fellow with the wine gave me a few swallows which started my drinking for the day.

One of the soldiers then said to me, "Hey, the General wants to see you."

I said, "Why would the General want to see me? What did I do, bomb his house or something.

But he said, "Come on. I'll take you to the General." It wasn't too far because I had landed in the backyard of the house taken over by the two top Generals in the Canadian Army; General Hoffmeister and General Burns!

Spitfire Comments

A dream. A real dream. It was great at every height and could out-turn and out-dive the Jerry fighters. The 109's and 190's couldn't turn and dive like the Spit could.

The British kept modifying the Spitfire to make it better but the only real outside difference was the nose; they just kept making it longer. The Germans had trouble identifying each version. The Spit V could be beaten by the 109 and 190 fighters. The Spit VIII could beat the 109, and the Spit IX could beat the 190. The Jerries didn't know what hit them. The armament, two 20mm cannons and four .303's, was certainly more than adequate.

Did you know you could almost hit the speed of sound in a dive with a Spitfire? It would shake like crazy, but would still hang together. If you tried that with any other plane back then, the wings would probably break off.

F/O Buzz Hayden
RCAF
J88723

417 Fighter Squadron being briefed before an 'op' in Italy.
— *Buzz Hayden (RCAF)*

Damage to German truck by incendiary cannon shells of 417 Squadron Spitfires.

'417' Spitfire landing at Anzio, Italy, on steel-matted runway.
— Buzz Hayden (RCAF)

Ground crew working on Spitfires. Brand new AN-L, in foreground is having its guns tested before F/O Buzz Hayden gets it. It's the aircraft in which he was later shot down.
—Buzz Hayden (RCAF)

A Mosquito after take-off

THE NIGHT INTRUDER
—one man's story of a mission over a German fighter field

Many years have gone by since I was engaged in Night Intruder operations over enemy territory during World War II. This number of years can do a lot to erase or dim memories, both good ones and bad. However, I have kept many notes and records made at the time I was doing this flying and these are complete enough to make 1944 seem like yesterday. Come back in time with me and share some of the feelings as we do an actual sortie together.

We are stationed on an airfield in England close to a small Norfolk town called Fakenham, at an even tinier hamlet called Little Snoring. My navigator, Paul Beaudet, and I are an experienced Mosquito crew with 23 Squadron, RAF, which shares this base with another RAF Intruder Squadron, 515.

Our base commander is G/C Sammy O'Brien-Hoare, DSO and Bar, DFC and Bar; and our commanding officer is W/C Sticky Murphy, DSO and Bar, DFC and Bar, Croix-de-Guerre and Palm, and Czech Medal.

Sammy Hoare pioneered our work in World War II and Sticky Murphy made a name for himself in dropping off and picking up undercover agents, flying Lysanders into occupied France and landing after dark without lights.

Paul and I have done thirty-eight trips since we started operating on July 12, 1944, and now we waken to a lovely November day, ready to get to work having had just a day off.

We are flying the British-built de Havilland Mosquito Mk VI fighter-bomber armed with four 20mm cannons, four .303 machine guns and two 500-pound bombs. The aircraft are painted the traditional grey-and-green camouflage and also sport the very stunning black-and-white invasion stripes on the under surfaces. Our exhaust stacks are shrouded to make us less visible to enemy night-fighters and we are equipped with Gee boxes which made it possible for us to determine our exact position over blacked-out Britain and to a lesser degree just inside enemy-held territory. We also carry a small black box called IFF (Identification Friend or Foe) and when we switch it on, our radar bashers can recognize us by our distinctive blip. We also had a destructive charge ready to detonate and destroy our IFF if there was any risk of the aircraft falling into enemy hands.

Canadian airmen operated on a two-tour system. In Night Intruder work the first tour would consist of thirty-five sorties followed by a period usually as instructors at operational units or in operational planning at group headquarters. A second tour of twenty-five trips would round out our operational obligation and we would be eligible for a posting home.

Paul and I did our first tour in eleven weeks and we were still raring to go, so we applied for and were granted an extension to our first tour of fifteen trips. We thought that by being very extra quiet about it we would be able to sneak in an extra ten sorties without anyone noticing and we could say that we'd done our two tours and get back home sooner. This plan didn't work and as soon as we finished the extra fifteen trips we were off operations. But for now let's get on with today's trip.

This is November 4, 1944, and Charlie, our batman, has just come into our Nissen hut with a cup of tea for us. He says, "Good morning, gentlemen. It is now 7:30 and we are having a nice day."

Tea is quite a ritual by now and it certainly warms you on a cold morning in an equally cold Nissen hut which is always cold and damp. There is no running water so we quickly wash in basins and put on our 'battle dress' and are ready to cycle over to the officers' mess about a mile away.

As a general rule of thumb we would operate two nights in a row, then a night off and a week's leave every six weeks. Paul and I decided that we would rather do three nights on, then one night off. We found that we were a bit edgy on the first night, alert on the second night, and except for being a bit tired we were fine for the third night's work.

Six or eight of us cycled to the mess just in time to enjoy our scrambled eggs and sausages and loads of tea with toast and jam, all generously mixed with conversation about last night's flying, any joy (damage to the enemy), anyone missing, etc.

The notice board in the mess has briefing time posted for 14:00 hours, leaving a few unrushed hours ahead to comfortably fit in all we have to do. The CO and flight commanders have left to go out to our flight offices and gradually we all mount our trusty bikes to follow them out there.

The aircraft status report is drawn up showing which aircraft are available today and which ones are, for any reason, not serviceable. Our flight commander has listed beside the aircraft registration the names of the on-duty crews and Paul and I note that we are again assigned Mosquito PZ448 YP-J, which happens to be our own regular kite.

Our aircraft has been topped up with fuel, oil, glycol and ammunition and since we didn't fly yesterday we prepare to do our traditional NFT (Night Flying Test); a short hop to give us the feel of the aircraft which often reveals some little snag that can be fixed up before our op. The Mossie is such a delightful aircraft to fly that we look forward to any excuse that would allow us to fly her—a pilot's dream!

With briefing called for 14:00 hours all aircrew and people involved, such as meteorology and intelligence bashers, flight commanders and CO's, head for the squadron intelligence library and briefing room behind station headquarters. The on-duty aircrews wait in the intelligence library until the planning is completed and usually there is a lot of speculation going on about where tonight's raid will be directed; plus the expected amount of armchair quarterbacking.

The orderly officer has just opened the door to the briefing room and that is our signal to file in. It is a large room, something like a classroon with a slightly elevated stage at the front, behind which, on the wall, is a large map of Europe. The target board is just off to one side of the stage and, as expected, we find it is covered.

S/L Charlie Price, our senior intelligence officer, has now mounted the podium and a hush fills the room. "Good afternoon, gentlemen; today's briefing will now begin. Will you please close the door, orderly officer, and I will call the roll."

He calls the names of each crew operating tonight and we answer "Sir" when he says, "F/O Stewart and F/O Beaudet."

Charlie has retired to the back of the stage and with his pointer he tells us which target our heavy bombers are pranging tonight, how many are being used and the routes to and from the target. He mentions the tactical purpose of the raid, such as demolition of certain industries or the demoralizing saturation bombing of a large city. He tells us about other groups supporting the raid, such as Pathfinders, and then he explains how we are going to be deployed. Our aircraft will be used to patrol enemy night-fighter aerodromes near the target and on the way to and from the raid.

At last the target board is uncovered and we all quickly look for our names, then our target and finally our patrol times. Charlie reads each one out and makes certain that the crew concerned understands clearly his job, his target, his patrol time, his armament and whether or not he is carrying two 500-pound bombs.

"Stewart and Beaudet, you are to patrol Ardorf Aerodrome from 20:15 hours until 21:15 and you will carry bombs. If you have time, take a look at Marx and Varez while you are in the area. Is that clear?"

"Yes, Sir."

The meteorology basher has his turn, telling us about tonight's winds and weather and usually we have lots of both. He tells what moonlight we can expect and gives us an idea of the weather at base upon our return. Tonight is no exception and we are warned about very strong winds.

Charlie Price has now asked W/C Sticky Murphy to say a few words. "All right, chaps, you know what you are expected to do; get cracking. Use your heads and don't stick your necks out. Be sure to keep a sharp lookout behind and watch out for that wind to change direction and strength!"

Charlie says, "Gentlemen, we will now synchronize our watches, half a minute before 14:56. I'll begin counting at ten seconds to go—ten, nine, eight, seven, six, five, four, three, two, one; 14:56—good luck, chaps!"

Mass briefing thus concluded each Mosquito crew pairs off to plan its own particular sortie since each operates independent of the other.

Paul has started to spread out his maps, his log, Dalton navigational computer—not to be confused with computers as we know them today, but a visual calculator—and Douglas protractor. My job is to draw flying rations, including enemy colours of the period (ESN's) so that we can fire them from our Very pistols if need be. These are nicknamed 'sisters'. I also draw escape kits in which we find small compasses, German aircraft cockpit checks on rice paper, concentrated food portions, first aid materials, water purifying tablets and pills to keep us awake.

I pull out the files on Ardorf, Marx and Varel aerodromes and note their layouts and remember where their defences are marked, as well as station buildings, ammo dumps, etc. I note, too, the heights of nearby obstructions. The main function and type of aircraft used in these places are night-fighting Ju-88's. I also draw out our phoney passport pictures and negatives. Paul has by now drawn in his tracks to our target and I note that we will cross the Dutch coast at Noord Egmond at 1,500-2,000 feet, diving and weaving from 3,500 feet. We are going to cruise at 240 MPH indicated air speed, starting out at 6,000 feet over base and steering 102 degrees magnetic. Our true air speed works out to be 260 MPH and with this wind our ground speed will be 310 MPH. Therefore 23 miles in four and a half minutes to the British coast where we will dive quickly to 500 feet over the English Channel and head for Noord Egmond, 134 miles and 31 minutes away, with a ground speed of 262 MPH.

Weaving over the Dutch coast, Paul and I will cruise on to our target, varying height from about 2,000 to 4,000 feet, keeping a constant lookout behind for any Ju-88's or Focke-Wulf 190's on our tails. Our next turning point is on the Leda River, southwest of Emben, then we turn into the patrol area just above the Jade Canal which leads into Wilhelmshaven. If Ardorf isn't lit or is hard to locate we may have to continue on to the north coast, pinpoint our location and backtrack to our target. We add up the anticipated times including this latest possibility and find that we have 75 minutes. Subtracting that from our slated time on target of 20:15, we know we must be off the ground at 19:00 hours. Our trip is planned; all we have to do is to fly it!

Paul has put all of his gear into his locker and we cycle over to the mess just in time for tea at 16:00 hours. We will miss dinner at the regular sitting because we are flying so early and so we gorge ourselves with tea, toast and cake.

Thus sated, we don our red goggles to adjust our 'visual purple' for night vision and relax for an hour, reading or chatting. The first emotion a crew feels at a time like this is the expectation that this sortie could mean joy, death or a cold jump into the night and a very uncertain future. Until it's time to go, we feel slightly cold and alone, our beds down at our hut seem to us to be so warm and enticing.

To all outward appearances the aircrew here in the mess are very offhanded about the whole thing and the impression we might give is that we couldn't care less—not so! We don't sit down and dread what's to be done. It's fascinating work and, as we do it, it's fun and very exciting at times.

"Well, Paul," I say, "It's 5:45. We'd better get down to the aircraft."

At our lockers by the flight office, we crawl into our escape boots and don our Mae Wests. I sign out and we pile into the fifteen-hundredweight van which takes us around the perimeter track to our dispersal area and aircraft. I walk over to Chiefy's office and sign the L-14 and then back to the aircraft.

Out there in the cool darkness it's like a world of our own. It all seems so unreal, so quiet, so private. Usually by this time a certain amount of anxiety has crept into our souls and down our spines and often has the effect of making us a bit high strung and cranky. It causes us to shiver slightly even though we don't feel cold. Usually silence prevails.

Now we come to our much-practised ritual before an operation: that of walking back to the tail of the aircraft to christen the tailwheel with urine for good luck!

With fifteen minutes to go we climb aboard, telling the ground crews to douse their flashlights because they'll spoil our night vision. We strap in; our ladder is removed, collapsed, and handed to Paul, who snaps it in its place on the door, after the door is closed and latched. The external starting batteries are plugged in, the engines are primed and we are ready to start. The odd few minutes before starting drag like hours. Eight minutes before take-off, I yell, "Contact starboard!" And we start our engines.

With both engines going and the radio heating up, we feel much better and our anxiety fades. The ground crew has unscrewed the undercarriage locks and removed the starting batteries, and they wave us out to the perimeter track where we follow the bluelights around to the take-off position. After I do a quick run-up and cockpit check, I flash our downward recognition light to signal that we are ready to go. A green light is flashed from the control-tower and we line up and take off.

All signals before an op are visual only so that the enemy can't tell by radio chatter when we depart. It's pretty black outside now and we don't feel too comfortable until we have 1,000 feet under us. the aircraft feels quite 'logy' with full 50-gallon drop tanks plus the outside weight of two 500-pound bombs. It is 19:00 hours and as we climb and turn to set course over the field, I flash . . . . V as we pass over.

The time is 19:06 and at 5,000 feet over Haisborough we alter course slightly for Noord Egmond, diving to 500 feet and switching off our navigation lights. It is fascinating to see the brightness of the phosphorescence in the water below us. On a black night like this it really shows up!

"Four minutes to go George," says Paul. This is my signal to climb quickly to 3,000-4,000 feet, ready to dive and weave our way across the Dutch coast just ahead. We can hear the enemy scanning us almost as soon as we climb; it sounds 'insect-like' in our earphones and it imparts a nervousness all of its own.

Diving and gently weaving we are safely across and level off between 1,500 and 2,000 feet. The scanning has stopped now and we set course for our next turning point. Flying along like this over enemy territory we see the odd rotating beacon and distant searchlight, and as we pass over the Zuider Zee we can see the riding lights of many small fishing craft. There is our landfall now coming up on the east coast of the Zuider Zee and we alter course for our previously mentioned turning point on the Leda Canal. We can now rely only upon waterways as landmarks because everything else below is pitch black.

"Look back, Paul," I say, as I pull sharply up and Paul scans behind for enemy aircraft. We did see a Ju-88 on one trip when we did this.

"There's Zuidlaarder, George. We are right on track," says Paul. "Let me know when you see the Dortmund Ems Canal."

We are soon there and shortly afterwards arrive at the turning point on the Leda River. I hum a few bars of 'What a lovely way to spend an evening' and Paul makes a rude comment.

"OK George, steer 005 and look out for the Jade Canal."

"OK Paul, have a look behind."

Five minutes later, over the Jade Canal, we can see ahead of us the landing pattern of lights that the Germans use to guide their aircraft in for a landing. It is Ardorf, nicely lit up to welcome us, right on the money at 20:15 hours.

"OK Paul, load up a 'sister' just in case we need it."

I dive the Mossie to 500 feet so that we can look up and see any aircraft silhouetted in the gloom. Paralleled searchlights challenge aircraft on the downwind leg with one holding and the other dipping.

"There goes an ESN (sister), Paul. Someone is on the downwind leg."

We race around the circuit and see some navigation lights on the final approach. Turning my gun safety switch to the firing position, we close in on him as he turns his landing lights on and we get a quick shot at him as he silhouettes himself against his own light. It's a Ju-88. Strikes appear on him all around the nose area and by now he must be very low.

Suddenly, the whole field is plunged into total blackness, as Paul and I speed up and around the airfield. Imagine our surprise when, looking up, we see another aircraft on the downwind leg. I pull up sharply and overshoot his tail, execute a sharp wing-over and close in to fire a quick burst of cannon at him, noticing strikes all over the starboard wing and cockpit area, and pieces falling off. It is a Heinkel 111 and there are huge sparks trailing behind as we pass. We see him no more.

We hang around the area for a while and keep getting challenged by the searchlights. One such time we fire off a 'sister' and the lights are doused.

"There goes their Visual Lorenz (the landing pattern of lights) on again, Paul" I say. As our patrol time is coming to an end I turn away, and quietly climb to 6,000 feet, ready to dive back in to bomb. Very often they will switch off all lights as we increase power to climb because they know what's coming.

OK, we're there now, and our bomb doors are open. Our bombs are armed and we roll into our dive, aiming at the runway—5,000 . . . . 4,000 . . . . 3,500. We ease out of the dive at 3,000 feet and release our bombs just as the searchlights reach up to grab us; we weave and skid gently out of the rays, looking to see our bomb strikes. We notice, too, that there is an extra string of lights beside the main flare path, and a lot of activity at the upwind threshold of the runway; that must be where our Ju-88 went in. There are our bomb bursts right on the runway. All lights now are doused as we weave and dive away from the airfield and set course for home.

"OK George, steer 293 degrees M. We're going for a Gee fix in the North Sea. ETA 22 minutes, 76 miles away against a headwind." This I do, and now we can both relax a bit.

At 21:35 hours we reach our invisible destination and Paul says, "OK George, alter course to 263 degrees M."

I say, "OK Paul, look behind."

We are headed for the British coast, 204 miles, 61 minutes away, and fatigue has caught up with me. I say to Paul, "Hang on to this for a bit while I rest my eyes, will you please?" So he reaches over and flies with his left hand as I lean my head back to rest. I sometimes wonder as I lean back like this if I will be alert enough to land the aircraft safely; I'm so tired now and we will start to accumulate a film of salt on our windscreen which will further reduce my visibility.

We are now forty miles from the British coast which is near enough to make our initial radio contact and, as Paul turns on our IFF, I say, "Hello, Largetype, this is Cricket 34, identifying, and my cockerel is crowing." That means that the IFF is turned on.

They reply, "Roger 24, Largetype out."

Ten minutes later, as we cross the coast, I transmit, "Cricket 34 drying my feet and changing frequencies."

"Roger 34, goodnight."

"Goodnight Largetype, and thank you. Cricket 34 out."

Now is the time to call base (Little Snoring), turn on my navigation lights and turn off my IFF.

"Hello Exking, Cricket 34 drying my feet, clear to circuit."

"Hello 34, you are clear to circuit. Call overhead at 3,000 feet."

"Roger Exking, 34 out." England is very black at that moment and it seems so unlikely that in all the darkness an airfield can suddenly light up.

"George," Paul says, "we are just coming over base now."

"Hello Exking, Cricket 34 over base at 3,000 feet. May we have the flare path lit, please?"

"Roger 34, Exking out."

Now I descend quickly to 1,500 feet on our downwind leg, drop the undercarriage, check my fuel, RPM, radiator flaps open, then turn smoothly to port on final, keeping my airspeed at 150

MPH all the way round. At 500 feet above the ground, full fine pitch, I drop my flaps, trim off the control pressures, and adjust power to hold 140 MPH and a nice sink rate. The threshold of the runway is coming up quickly now. I allow my speed to slacken to 130 as I cross. Then, throttling right back, we sink gently to touch down with the tail wheel low; not a three-pointer, but much smoother and always in control.

Turning off at the end of the runway I call, "Cricket 34 clear. Goodnight."

To which our controller replies, "Roger 34. Goodnight, old chap."

I taxi along the perimeter track to our dispersal area where the ever-faithful ground crew has been standing by for our return. We are guided into position by our marshaller waving his illuminated wands. Brakes on, engines at 1,000 RPM, radio off, red flaps closed, pull out the idle cut-off knobs and, when both props are stopped; gas off, switches off, throttles closed and all lights off.

Paul opens the door, hands down our ladder and prepares to disembark. The ground crew says, "Chocks in place." Then, "Any joy?"

"A bit," I say. "Brakes off."

Paul is now climbing down the ladder and the gyros are still humming as I unstrap and remove my helmet. "Ouch!" My bloody ears hurt from the damned earphones pressing against them and my face is tender and perspiring where my oxygen mask has been touching it. What a relief to get it all off. My bottom is now feeling the effects of sitting on a most uncomfortable dinghy for so long, and as I climb down, my circulation starts up again, and I long to stretch. This I do as soon as I get out, taking a much savoured deep breath and head back to re-christen our tailwheel before the fifteen-hundredweight arrives—often with a WAAF driver—to take us back to the flight office and our lockers.

We are now feeling very slap-happy with fatigue and happiness to be back, and we laugh at anything and everything as we chat with our ground crew and then with other crews on the way.

Back at the intelligence section with a cup of hot tea and a cookie, we relax and wait to be debriefed and all at once the world seems to be a better place. The intelligence officer motions us over to a seat and we tell him all about our trip as he makes notes and, this soon concluded, we hand in our escape kits, retrieve our valuables and head for the officers' mess, where with the other crews we have a most welcome meal of eggs and bacon, and toast and tea. There is lots of chatter as we linger over this treat and then delicious fatigue creeps over all of us and we gradually break up, and bike back to our huts, tired but relaxed and happy.

(A special thanks to the author, George Stewart for his NIGHT INTRUDER article which had been previously published in the Canadian Aviation Historical Society's book called I'LL NEVER FORGET, a 1977 publication.)

Mosquito Comments

Fantastic! It was versatile, maneuverable, and had the armament. When I flew the Mosquito, it was considered the fastest aircraft in the world. I loved every minute of it!

The serviceability was great; I flew one for 100 hours and the only repair was a Pesco pump.

F/O George Stewart
RCAF
J24403